Tommy Emmanuel's

FINGERSTYLEGUITAR
MILESTONES

Master Fingerstyle Guitar Technique with Virtuoso Tommy Emmanuel, CGP

TOMMY**EMMANUEL**

TRUEFIRE

FUNDAMENTAL**CHANGES**

Tommy Emmanuel's Fingerstyle Guitar Milestones

Master Fingerstyle Guitar Technique with Virtuoso Tommy Emmanuel, CGP

ISBN: 978-1-78933-012-0

Published by **www.fundamental-changes.com**

Copyright © 2020 TrueFire LLC

Edited by Joseph Alexander & Tim Pettingale

Over 13,000 fans on Facebook: **FundamentalChangesInGuitar**

Instagram: **FundamentalChanges**

For over 300 Free Guitar Lessons with Videos Check Out

www.fundamental-changes.com

Cover Image Copyright: Tommy Emmanuel, used by permission.

Special thanks to Levi Clay and Daryl Kellie for their assistance.

Contents

About the Author

Tommy Emmanuel is a virtuoso guitarist, composer, educator and musical innovator who has a career spanning over four decades. He has released many award-winning albums and has gained widespread industry respect and recognition.

Tommy has topped *Guitar Player* and *Music Radar* magazine's "Best Acoustic Guitarist" poll. He was voted *Rolling Stone* (Australia) Magazine's "Most Popular Guitarist" for two consecutive years. He has earned four Platinum and Gold albums, two consecutive "Golden Guitar" awards (2006, 2007) at the CMAA Awards in Australia, and has won two Aria Awards (Australia's Grammys). Tommy performed with his brother Phil at the Sydney 2000 Olympics closing ceremony, which was viewed by over 2 billion people around the world.

In July 1999, at the 15th Annual Chet Atkins Appreciation Society Convention, Chet presented Tommy with his Certified Guitar Player Award (CGP) – an honor he bestowed on just four guitarists. Chet said, "He is one of the greatest guitar players I've ever seen." Tommy performs at the Chet Atkins Appreciation Society (CAAS) in July each year in Nashville.

A two-time Grammy nominee, Tommy has become renowned for his "one-man band" guitar technique, simultaneously threading together bass, chords, melody and rhythmic percussive hits. His gifts have won him many accolades in the guitar world and in his native Australia, where he was made a Member of the Order of the Australia – an honor bestowed by Queen Elizabeth II.

For more information visit: **http://tommyemmanuel.com/about/**

Get the Video

Enhance your learning experience!

Thank you for buying this book. To take your learning experience to the next level, we are delighted to give readers a special discounted offer on the interactive video version of *Tommy Emmanuel's Fingerstyle Milestones*, which this book is based on.

In the video version, Tommy presents over 2 hours of multi-angle video lessons, featuring performances and detailed breakdowns. Viewing angles include wide angle, right-hand, left-hand and composite views. Close-ups of the fretting and picking hands mean that you'll quickly nail the essential techniques and be on your way to discovering the wonders of polyphonic guitar playing – Tommy-style.

Tommy also takes full advantage of TrueFire's interactive learning tools to put everything you need at your fingertips: a multi-angle interactive video lesson player features looping, zooming, video-tab sync, Guitar Pro files and other handy learning tools and controls.

For the complete learning experience, head over to **https://truefire.com/fundamental** and use CODE: THRILLSEEKER to sign-up for a free account, or scan the QR code below:

Once your account is created, you'll have access to the special offer to purchase and download the entire video course.

Introduction

Hi there Thrill Seekers!

I'm tremendously excited to take you on a journey to teach you the fundamentals of fingerstyle guitar – *my way* – from the ground up. You're in for an awesome ride, so grab your guitar and buckle up. This trip might just change your life!

Throughout my career, I've met and taught thousands of guitarists of all different levels. The biggest thing I've realized is that playing great fingerstyle guitar is all about getting the basics right as early as possible. In this book, I'll teach you the fundamental elements of fingerstyle guitar and quickly help you to use them to play thrilling pieces of music.

Learning fingerstyle is a series of milestones and the most important are the early ones, where you learn the skills of thumb and finger independence in your picking hand. This hand is the engine, the powerhouse of everything you play. We will spend some time building control and independence between your thumb and fingers. Once that's in place, everything else becomes so much easier.

There's a rhythmic logic to picking hand technique which runs through all fingerstyle guitar music, no matter how complex. Whether you want to play like Merle Haggard, Chet Atkins or Jerry Reed, or if you want to play folk, classical or bluegrass, the picking technique is what drives the music. Once mastered, you can apply it to any style of music you choose.

What you *won't* find in this book are hundreds of boring technical exercises. I believe in developing great technique while learning *actual* music. Every example in this book naturally builds toward playing real pieces of exciting music that you'll enjoy and get satisfaction from performing. I break down the pieces into their most important components, then show you how to put them all together.

Each of the study pieces in this book is broken down for you into essential techniques, concepts, etudes and musical exercises that build and combine magically into complete songs. By the end you will not only have a tremendous sense of achievement, you'll also be able to dazzle and impress your friends!

Thumb control

The first part of building the picking hand is to develop independence in the thumb. The thumb creates the familiar "boom chick" rhythm of country music and is responsible for all the wonderful basslines you hear played by the fingerstyle masters. Often, students don't spend enough time mastering the thumb because they want to skip forward onto more complicated ideas. This is always a mistake and one of the biggest stumbling blocks for developing players. Developing your picking thumb technique is the most important thing you can do before moving on.

Finger independence

Once your thumb is under control, it's time to start adding in the other fingers of the picking hand. First, we'll add plucked chords on the beat. Next, we'll introduce syncopated (offbeat) ideas. This is a lot of fun and extremely satisfying. When you can confidently combine your fingers and thumb, you'll not only be a solid fingerstyle player, you'll be able to accompany other musicians and work with singers easily. I've included loads of short etudes to help you develop these skills in a musical environment.

Making music

When you've developed independence in your picking hand, it's time to play some full songs. I'll show you exactly how I go about learning new songs and making them musical. As we explore the music, we'll come across new techniques that will allow you to add fretting hand melodies to your chord progressions, all while playing the thumb and finger patterns you developed earlier. I'll teach you to add hammer-ons and pull-offs to enhance your arrangements and combine everything into meaningful music.

While the techniques in this section are a little more challenging, they're used on almost every song you'll learn, so once mastered you'll have access to a whole new world of possibilities.

Work hard and have fun

I've designed this course to help you get to grips with fingerstyle guitar in a fun, friendly and rewarding way. I'm sure you're going to love it, but you're going to have to practice. Nothing in life comes for free. As guitar players we pay our dues in the practice room or woodshed. I'll give you tips on practicing effectively throughout the book.

And finally…

Before we get started, remember that learning fingerstyle guitar is just like walking, talking or catching a ball – a great deal of it is about developing *muscle memory*, especially in the picking hand. The movement of your picking hand must gradually become unconscious, so you need to program it *slowly* and *accurately*. When you're confident, speed up each exercise/song bit by bit, using a metronome. There are no shortcuts, but I promise you that you'll find the results rewarding.

OK, enough chat! Let's get started by looking at some of the gear you'll need to play fingerstyle guitar.

Good luck and have fun.

Tommy

Get the Audio

The audio files for this book are available to download for free from **www.fundamental-changes.com.** The link is in the top right-hand corner. Simply select this book title from the drop-down menu and follow the instructions to get the audio.

We recommend that you download the files directly to your computer, not to your tablet, and extract them there before adding them to your media library. You can then put them on your tablet, iPod or burn them to CD. On the download page there is a help PDF, and we also provide technical support via the contact form.

For over 350 Free Guitar Lessons with Videos Check out:

www.fundamental-changes.com

Over 13,000 fans on Facebook: **FundamentalChangesInGuitar**

Instagram: **FundamentalChanges**

Get your audio now for free:

It makes the book come alive, and you'll learn much more!

www.fundamental-changes.com/download-audio

Chapter One: Guitars, Gear and Mindset

"Fingerstyle guitar" is a catch-all title and there are many different types – each of which might suggest using a different type of guitar. Classical guitar is a type of fingerstyle that generally requires a specific instrument. Great jazz fingerstyle players like Martin Taylor tend to favor archtop guitars. Folk fingerstyle music generally utilizes steel string acoustics, and such greats as James Taylor and Don McLean have developed their own approaches to playing this style. Then, a great deal of country and bluegrass music is played fingerstyle, made famous by players such as Merle Haggard, Chet Atkins, Jerry Reed and others, who played it on all kinds of guitars!

The information above, and a lot of the advice you'll hear, might suggest that you need a certain kind of guitar to be able to play the music you'll learn in this book, but let me blow that myth out of the water right now. The *best* guitar for you is the one that you love playing. The one that feels comfortable to you because it's *just right*. It doesn't matter what name is on the headstock, where it was made, or how much it cost. If you love it, that's what's important.

That said, I would like to mention a couple of things.

First, there is one technical issue to consider when playing this sort of music:

Often, fingerstyle guitar players use the thumb of their fretting hand to reach over the top of the neck to fret the bass notes of a chord. This is a common technique and it's just easier on a steel string acoustic with a relatively slim neck. If you play a nylon string classical guitar, you'll find this technique more challenging with its wider neck and will potentially miss out on an important technique that will unlock a lot of fingerstyle repertoire.

However, you don't need to spend a fortune these days to acquire a good steel string guitar, and for anyone starting out in this style, it will be a good investment. Even budget instruments made by recognized brands are manufactured to a high standard. Guitars by well-proven makers such as Fender, Yamaha, Gibson, Maton, Martin, Taylor and Ibanez will be fine. If you can afford it, it's always best to invest a little more if you can, but it's by no means necessary.

Second, people ask me all the time about the guitars, strings, picks etc., that I prefer. While you don't need to replicate my gear to get the right sound, here's what I use:

Guitars

These days I play steel string acoustics made in Australia (like me!) by a wonderful company called Maton. The guys at Maton were kind enough to give me my own signature T.E. series. T.E. guitars really suit me as they feel great and the neck is lovely and thin.

Another reason why I don't use nylon string guitars is because I don't play with my nails. I play with the callouses I've developed on my fingers from years of fingerpicking. Some players grow their nails, some use stick-on acrylic nails; but because I use a combination of thumb pick and fingers, I find that the sound of a steel string guitar is right for me. I just love that twang!

Thumb picks

There are many different kinds of thumb picks available, but the kind I like to use are the thick, strong plastic ones made by Jim Dunlop. A lot of people recommend Fred Kellie thumb picks, but they're a bit too soft for me. You should try a few different types and find the one that works best for you. Play a few tunes with it in your local music store and make sure it's comfortable. Ensure that it's not loose – it shouldn't slip around on your thumb. But, equally, while it should fit tightly to your thumb, don't get one that's so tight it cuts off your circulation. Jerry Reed wrote the song *Blue Finger* after wearing a thumb pick that was too tight!

Here is another tip: the right thumb pick shouldn't be too long and will naturally sit comfortably on your thumb. If you find a pick that seems to be the right length, but the part that goes around your thumb is a bit loose, you can put the pick in hot water and reshape it slightly. Another trick is to use a bit of electrical tape around the pick to help tighten it around your finger.

There's also a lot to be said for playing fingerstyle without a thumb pick, in the style of Robert Johnson or Eric Clapton, if that's what feels more natural. Without a thumb pick, these players use their thumb to push almost straight through the string and create a funky edge to their sound.

Above all, experiment. We're all different as musicians and have different preferences. What works for me might not sound good to you – although I do urge you to try to get to grips with the thumb pick if you can, as it's a big part of creating that authentic sound.

Throughout this book, I will explain each example as if you were using a thumb pick, but feel free to make adjustments if you don't want to use one.

Tunings and string gauges

I use a fairly light gauge of 12-54 acoustic strings made by the guitar company Martin. I think they achieve a great balance between giving me a nice comfortable action (the height of the strings above the fretboard) and just enough weight to dig in hard and create the tone I love to hear.

Most of my songs are written in standard EADGBE tuning on the guitar. Often fingerstyle guitar is associated with alternate tunings like DADGAD or Open D tuning. A couple of my songs are written in the tuning DGDGBE (standard tuning with the lowest strings tuned down by a tone). This is a G6 chord with a D in the bass, which is something I stole from Chet Atkins. I wrote the songs *The Tall Fiddler*, *The Cowboy's Dream* and *The Mystery* using this tuning because I love it so much! However, each piece of music in this book is written in standard tuning, so you don't need to worry about other tunings for now.

Mindset

Lastly, I've written this book with three important goals for you in mind:

1. To truly understand the picking technique of fingerstyle guitar – and not only to understand it, but to learn to *feel* it as well.

2. To develop great independence between your thumb and fingers, treating them almost as two separate instruments. I'm going to show you lots of exercises to help you develop these skills.

3. To teach you some songs. Learning complete songs is so important because it gives you an incredible feeling of accomplishment and progression. You'll have something to show for all your effort and you'll be able to show people how far you've come. There's nothing quite like playing music to warm your soul.

Try to memorize everything you learn in this book, rather than keep referring back to the notation. It's important to commit this stuff to memory so you can perform it with passion and conviction. To do this, work on one small section at a time and repeat it until it's solid, then move on to the next short section. Repeat the next section until you can play it without any effort, then join it to the previous part. Now practice these two parts together before moving on to the next, and so on. Make repetition your mate! You need it to become a good musician and a great technician of the guitar.

Ultimately, it's up to you how good you want to get at fingerstyle guitar. That simply comes down to how dedicated you are and how much work you're willing to put in. Speaking for myself and a lot of my peers, we don't just love it, we are *consumed* by it. It's our life and passion. I'm hoping this fire can be lit in you too.

When you finish this book, your next goal is to seek out great songs that you love. Break them down, reverse engineer them and memorize their tiniest details. Not only will this teach you a great deal about the music itself, it will help you build a wonderful repertoire that you can sit and play with other musicians.

OK, I think we're ready to go! You've got your guitar, you've got your thumb pick, and you've got the right attitude... let's get to work!

Chapter Two: Deconstructing Boom Chick

In this chapter, we'll look at how we can achieve goal number one: to understand how the thumb works in fingerstyle and to get it working on its own, independently of the fingers. This takes time, so it's important to *go slowly*. You must do this correctly right from the start, so that you don't program your muscle memory with any bad habits.

We'll begin with some simple open chords: E, A and B7.

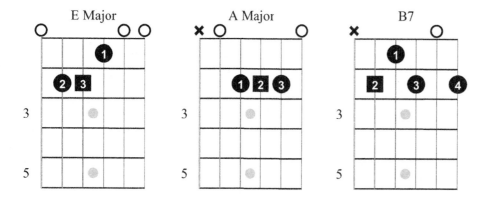

In my brand of fingerstyle guitar, there's an important rule you need to know:

The root of the chord is always played on the first beat of the bar.

This means that when playing an E chord, you will always play the E root note on beat one. With an A chord, you'll always play the A root note on beat one, and so on.

Here's a simple exercise that will help you map out the most common country fingerstyle chord sequence with just bass notes. This exercise will help you get used to using the thumb pick too. Hold down the full chord, but only pick the bass note.

Don't forget, this book comes with audio and it's really helpful to hear as well as visualize these exercises. You can grab it from **www.fundamental-changes.com**

Remember, you're using *only your thumb* to play the following exercises. I want you to rest all your other fingers on the guitar body under the strings. I stress this because it's amazing how players always want to add their fingers into the mix. In fact, when I teach private students, I've been known to stick their fingers to the guitar with gaffer tape! Keep the fingers still and only move the thumb. Make contact with the string using the end of the thumb pick, if you're using one, and keep the thumb straight and parallel to the strings.

Example 2a

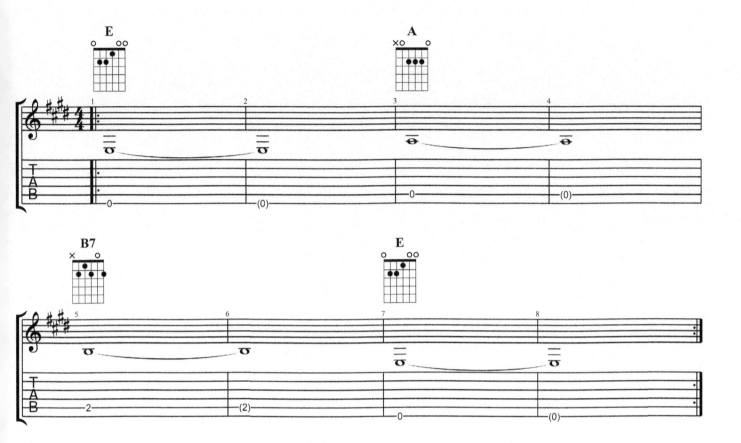

That's a great start, but let's develop your thumb picking a little further. In the following example, I want you to pick the lowest three strings of each chord in rhythm. Each note is played on a beat, so set a metronome to click at 60 beats per minute (bpm) and play one note per click with a rest on the fourth beat. If you're struggling, turn the metronome off until you start to get the hang of it.

Example 2b

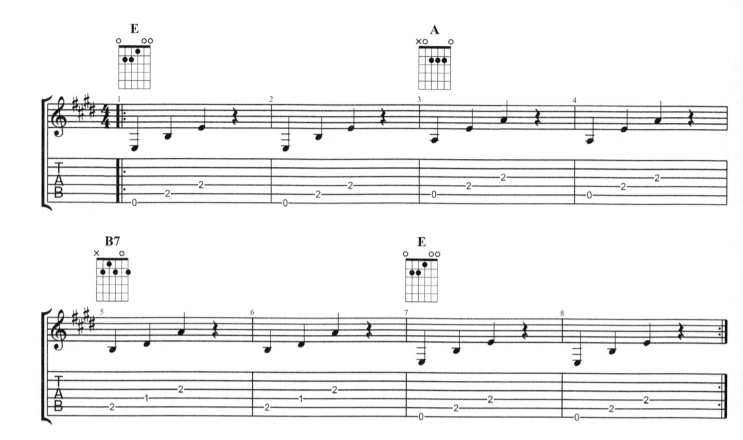

Now you're getting to grips with the basic picking movement, let's learn an important picking pattern you'll use in almost every song you play. We'll begin with the bass pattern we used on the E Major chord. The idea is to play root on the 6th string first (remember our rule), then the 4th string, the 5th string, and finally the 4th string again. It sounds like this:

Example 2c

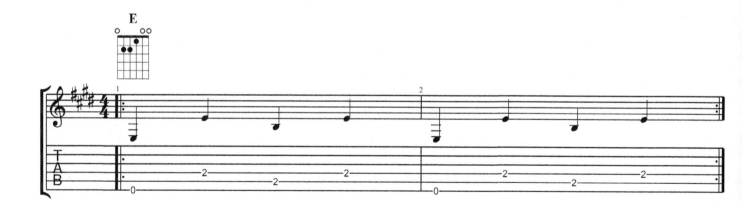

When we move to the A Major chord, the first note is an A, but the pattern is slightly different.

Example 2d

Finally, here's the B7 chord. Once again, the B root note is played on the first beat of the bar, but this pattern is a little trickier. The picking hand plays the same pattern as the A Major chord above, but you need to move your second finger across from the 2nd fret on the fifth string, to the 2nd fret on the 6th string on beat three. You start off in this position:

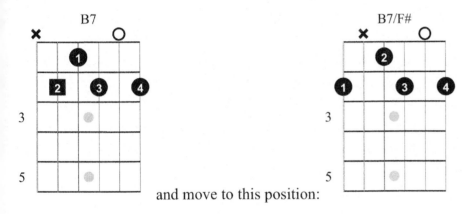

and move to this position:

Play along with the audio to make sure you're doing it right.

Example 2e

When you've mastered each of the three picking patterns, you can start to combine them into short pieces of music. Begin by moving from E Major to A Major.

Example 2f

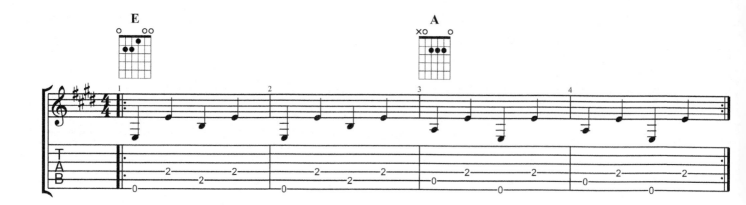

Now combine E Major and B7.

Example 2g

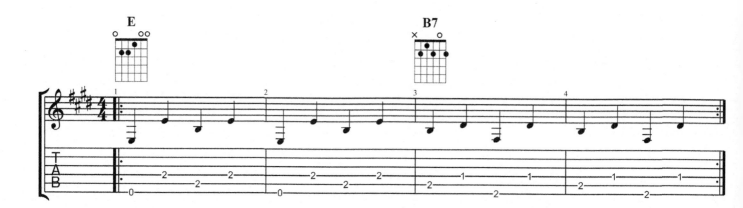

Finally, combine all three chords with this common progression.

Example 2h

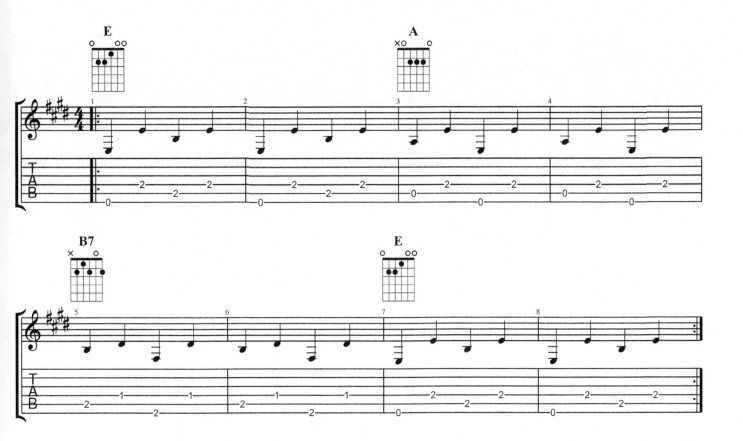

So far, we've concentrated on playing just one note at a time, but to create a real *boom chick* sound we want to play a couple of strings on every second beat. To begin with, you should play the following exercises accurately, as written, but as you progress you may wish to loosen up the picking hand and be less accurate with the "mini strums".

In the following example, you'll play an E chord. Play the first and third beats with a single pick, but add an extra string to the picks on beats two and four. By doing this you'll start to hear the classic boom chick sound emerge. Playing the extra note really helps to spell out what the chord is.

The thumb, and the angle of the thumb pick, should be parallel to the guitar strings to create a clean sound.

Example 2i

Repeat this process with the A Major and B7 chords before combining them together into a short sequence.

Example 2j

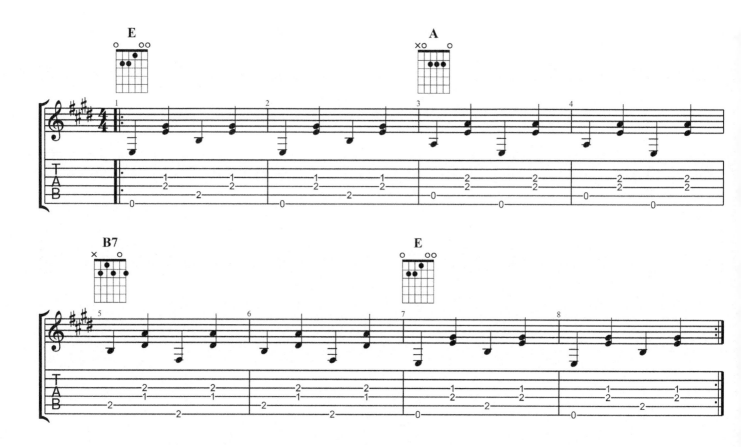

Now, you may be thinking to yourself, "That doesn't sound quite right – the notes are ringing too much!" And you'd be right.

The Palm Mute

The next stage in the development of our boom chick rhythm is to slightly mute the guitar strings with the picking hand. To do this, place the flesh of your picking hand gently on the bridge/saddle of the guitar, so that the flesh is just in contact with the strings. You should be able to play the picking pattern with ease while muting the strings. Here's Example 2j again, but this time with the picking hand muting the strings. Check it out in the audio example.

Example 2k

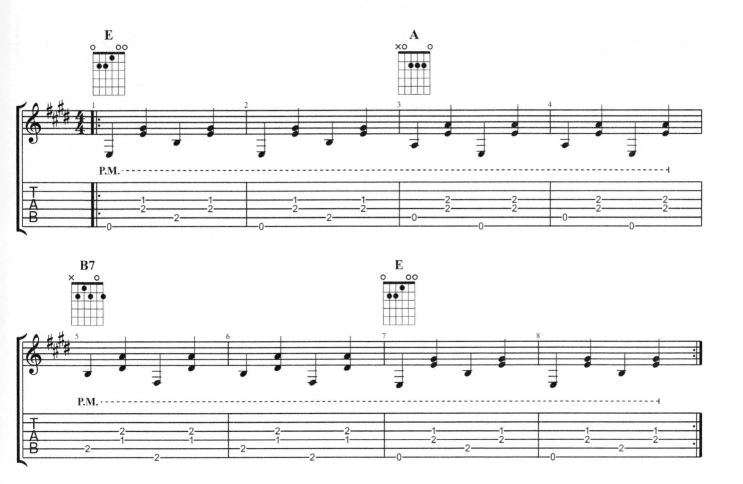

I'm sure you can hear what a difference palm muting makes. To test your ability to change chords smoothly, try the following sequence where each chord lasts for just one bar. Set your metronome to 60bpm and gradually increase the speed to 120bpm as your skills develop.

Example 21

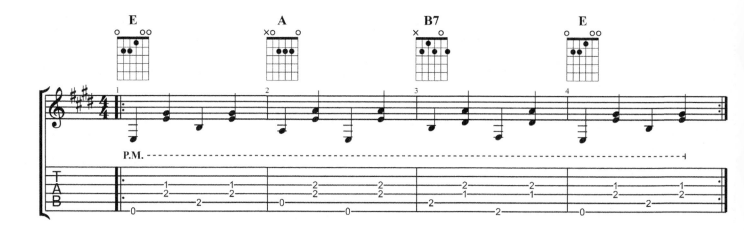

This is the very beginning of fingerstyle guitar playing. The palm muted bassline pattern with a mini-strum is foundational to everything we will do from now on. Learn this technique slowly and make sure you can play it smoothly while you change chords. Rhythm is very important, because you don't want any ugly gaps in the music while you change chords.

Before we move on to using the boom chick rhythm with other chords, I want to talk quickly about how I play my E Major chord. At the beginning of this chapter, I gave you a chord diagram for E Major that looked like this:

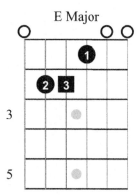

However, I normally don't finger the E Major chord like that. Instead, I use my second finger to play both the lower fretted notes like this:

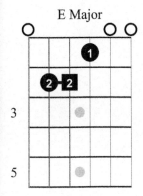

E Major

Not everyone can do this, but I play the chord this way to save a bit of energy and free up my other fingers to add melody notes later. If you can play E Major with my fingering, go for it. If not, don't worry, there's more than one way to skin a cat!

Boom Chick with Other Chords

As you know, there are more than three chords in music, so let's take a look at how we play the boom chick rhythm with some other common open position chords. First, C Major and G Major.

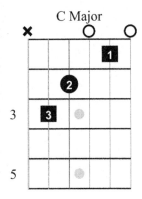

C Major

There are a few ways to play the G Major chord. I use both of the following fingerings, but most commonly I'll use a barre chord, which we'll come to later.

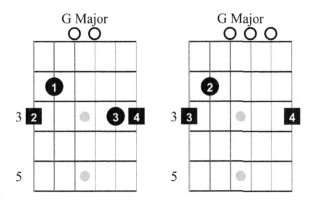

G Major   G Major

Let's put these chords into a progression. To keep the bassline going on C Major, you need to move the lowest finger from the fifth to the sixth string (just like the B7 chord earlier).

Example 2m

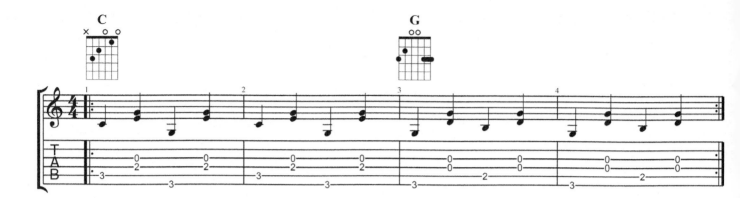

Now let's introduce F Major into the mix. F Major is one of those chords that is the bane of many a guitar player's life, because it requires a lot of effort to hold it down and sound it cleanly. The traditional way to play the chord is to use the first finger as a barre across the whole neck, which can be especially challenging for beginners.

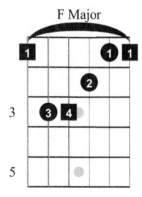

The way I play it, to make things easier, is to hook my thumb over the top of the neck to play the root note on the first fret like this (indicated by the T).

F Major

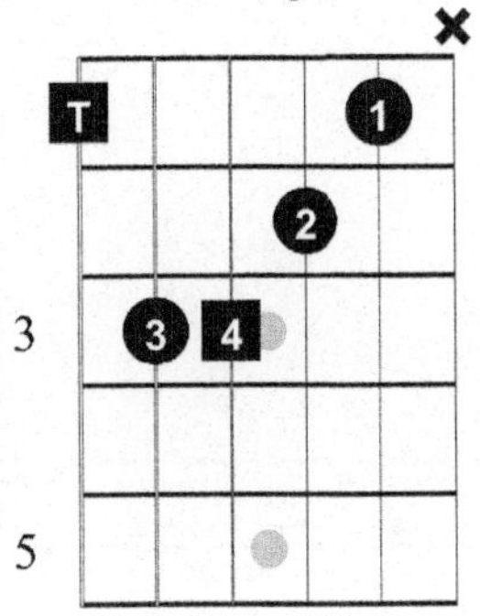

If you don't like either of those options, there's a third way. You can use your first finger to play the bass note and only play the E, A, D and G strings, so that you don't need to barre.

F Major

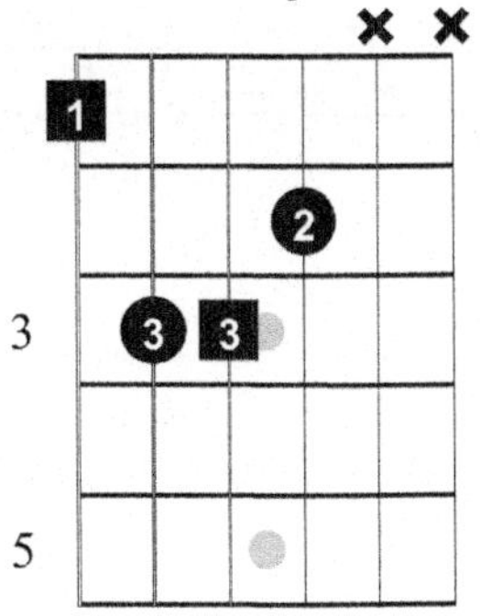

If you can, play it my way by hooking your thumb over the neck to play the bass note, because this will leave the fingers free for when we add melody notes on the top strings. If you can't manage that, go with whatever feels most comfortable for you.

These three ways to play F Major are all *movable voicings*. This means they can be slid up and down the guitar neck to create different chords. We'll look at this idea more in a minute. First, try this short etude that includes the F Major chord.

Example 2n

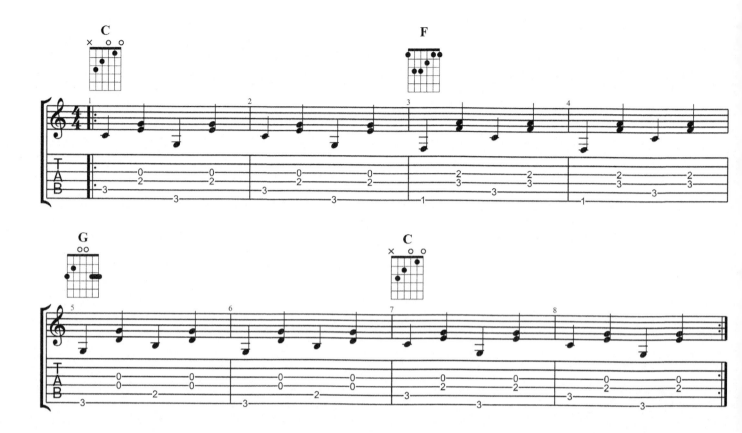

Now let's learn how to move from G Major to D Major.

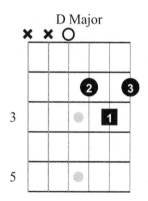

Example 2o

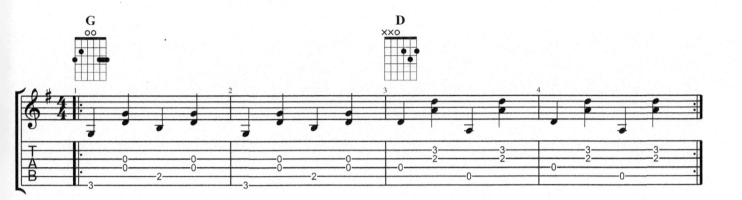

Sometimes, fingerstyle guitarists use their thumb to play D Major with the note F# (the 3rd) in the bass. It's a bit tricky to finger at first, but it means that you can use the same boom chick pattern on D Major and G Major.

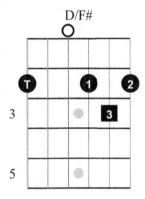

Try it now!

Example 2p

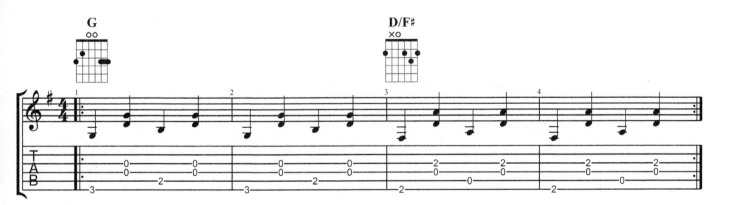

Here's a short etude that combines the chords G Major, C Major and D Major. Try the D Major with and without the thumb hooked over the top to play the F# in the bass.

Example 2q

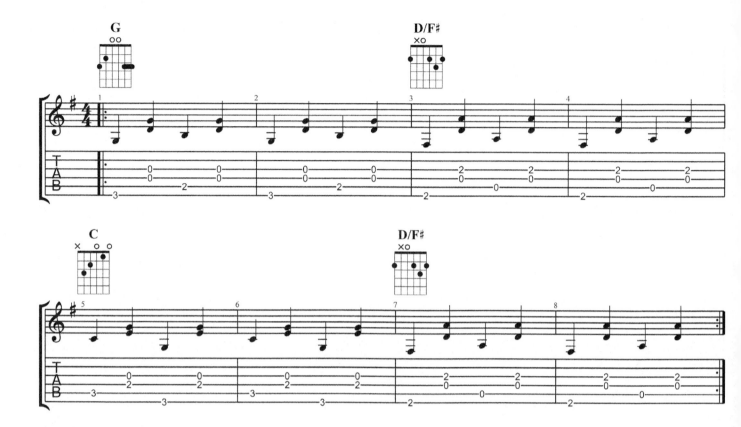

Now I want to talk to you a little bit more about barre chords. Quite often, I won't play the open position of the G Major chord. Instead, I'll use a barre chord and use my thumb to play the bass note. Try the next example using this fingering of G Major. It may take some practice, but if you can get into the habit of fretting bass notes with the thumb, it will help you later on.

G Major

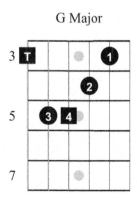

Example 2r

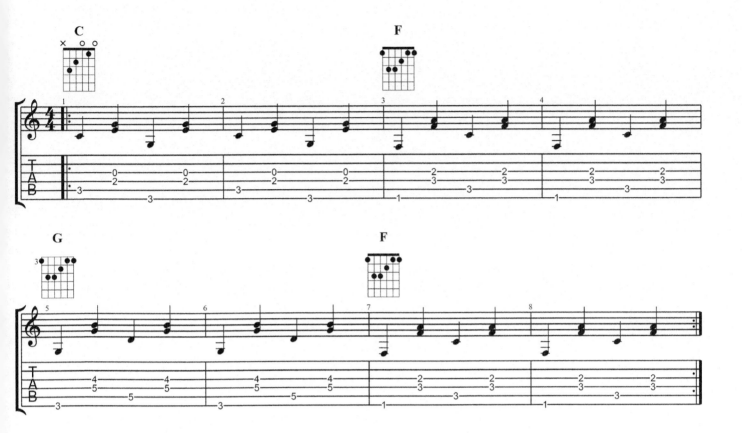

There are two more barre chords I want you to learn. When you know them, you'll be able to play almost any country-style blues in any key. The first is a barre chord with its root played on the fifth string. Use your pinkie finger to make the barre at the 5th fret.

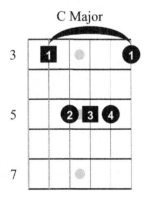

As with most chords with a root on the 5th string, you need to move the bass note between the fifth and sixth strings to create the boom chick rhythm. You may be thinking that you can permanently barre your first finger between the fifth and sixth strings to save energy, but don't! You'll get a much better sound if you move the first finger only when you have to. Try it now.

Example 2s

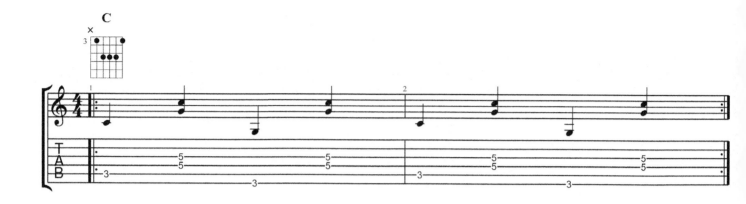

Try moving this pattern up the neck, two frets at a time while keeping the bass pattern going, to get used to the shape.

Example 2t

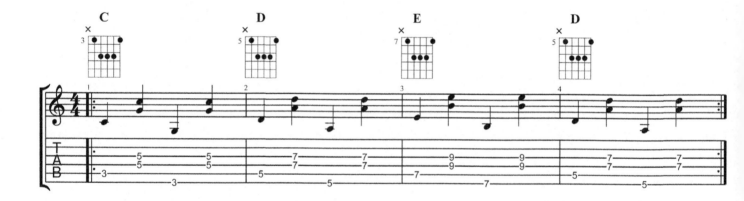

The final barre chord to learn is based around the open C Major chord. You should recognize the shape. Having a barre chord version of the C Major shape means we can move the chord up and down the neck and play in any key. We're going to play an E Major chord using this shape. It's fingered like this:

E Major

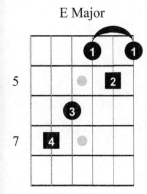

This time, to play the boom chick bassline, you'll need to move your pinkie finger back and forth between the fifth and sixth strings. This is a great exercise for strengthening the pinkie!

Don't forget to mute the strings with your picking hand to help create the boom chick rhythm.

Example 2u

Now it's time to combine three barre chord voicings into a short sequence and learn to move between them smoothly while keeping the boom chick rhythm going. Practice this one slowly to get accustomed to the new shapes. Let's play this one in Ab… are you ready?!

Example 2v

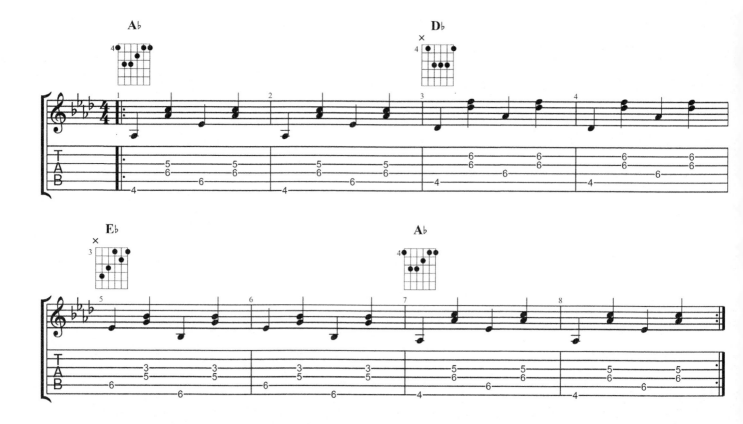

When you get the hang of them, these barre chords are great. They open up the neck and give us lots of possibilities later when we start to add melody to our rhythm parts.

Finally, it's important to know that there's another way to play the boom chick rhythm in the key of E by using a fragment of the C-shape barre chord you just learned.

In this example we will play through the sequence E Major, A Major, B Major and E Major using barre chords, but we'll play the bassline in a slightly different way.

Here's the fragment of the E Major barre chord that I want you to use. Place your first finger on the 4th fret.

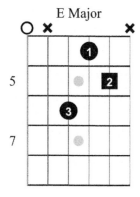

Then we will play the A Major chord with an open A string like this:

A Major

And we'll use a normal barre with a thumb in the bass for the B Major chord

B Major

Notice how I use my pinkie finger to play the bassline on the 7th fret of the sixth string on the E chord. For the A Major chord, I play the bassline with open strings, just as if it was a normal, open-position voicing.

Example 2w

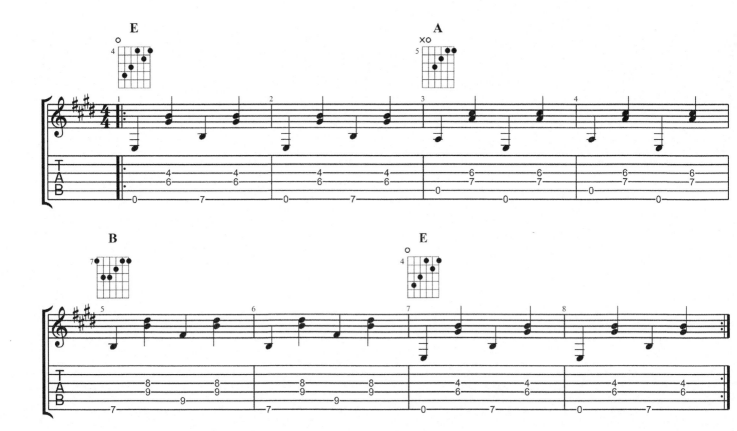

Well done! To get this far you've made a great deal of progress. I hope you're starting to see the potential of making music like this and are excited to continue your journey into fingerstyle guitar. Before we move on, I want you to do one more thing for me. Most of the examples in this chapter have been played with one chord held for two bars. Now go through every example and play them again, but this time with only one bar per chord. For example, instead of Example 2j being played like this…

…I want you to play it like this:

Example 2x

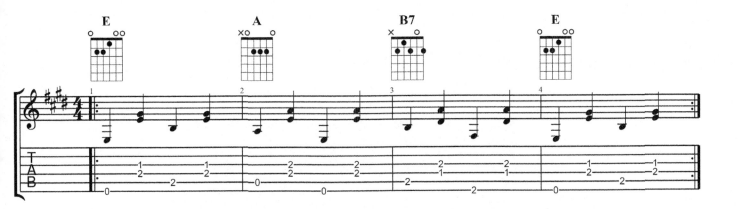

Don't move on until you can play everything in this chapter comfortably and the boom chick action is happening unconsciously.

There have been plenty of exercises in this first section, but I've done my best to make them all musical and useful. I'm sure you've heard a lot of chord sequences that you recognize from popular tunes and are ready to add a bit more rhythm to them. In the next chapter we are going to develop the independence between your thumb and fingers to help you do just that.

Chapter Three: Adding the Fingers

Now you've got your thumb firing on all cylinders, it's time to un-tape your digits from the guitar body and begin to develop the independence between your fingers and thumb.

You may find this section a little more complicated and a bit more challenging, but once you get to grips with these ideas, you're going to have a lot of fun. The techniques in this section are at the *heart* of all great fingerstyle playing. Once you put them into practice, not only will they give you a great deal of satisfaction, they will also teach you to become a great accompanist for singers and other musicians.

When I play fingerstyle guitar, the index and middle fingers on the picking hand are my *main* melody fingers. As Chet Atkins used to say, "A thumb and two fingers, he started to play," however, I do sometimes use my ring and pinkie finger, so there are no hard and fast rules. The most important consideration is to get the melody to *feel* and *sound* good.

To begin with, most of the exercises we'll do in this section are played with the thumb, index and middle fingers of the picking hand.

Picking hand position

I normally position my picking hand so that its fleshy heel is just above the saddle of the guitar. This allows me to mute the strings to achieve that solid *boom chick*. In this position, my straightened thumb reaches just over the sound hole and my picking fingers are in a natural position. I don't tend to pick notes where the fretboard meets the body, as some players do, because I'm not particularly in love with that sound.

I also anchor my pinkie finger to the guitar body to support my hand and help me move my fingers into the correct location. People love to argue with me about anchoring the pinkie, but I know it works! Ultimately, you'll always end up going your own way, but I ask you to try it my way for a while. The pinkie really does hold everything steady.

Here's a picture of my hand, mid-song, so you can see the position. Notice that my thumb is straight, my pinkie is anchored, and my melody fingers are nice and relaxed.

It may take a bit of time to make this position feel comfortable for you, but stick with it through the following exercises.

Developing finger and thumb independence

With your hand position sorted, here's an exercise that will help you to develop your first bit of independence. Refresh your memory with the picking pattern you played back in Example 2c. Here it is again to save you flicking back:

We're going to combine this bass pattern with a ringing chord played on beat one of the bar. To play this chord, use your index, middle and ring fingers to pick the top three strings.

Example 3a

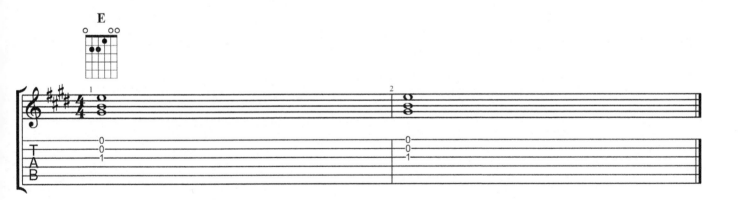

Now you know what your thumb and fingers are doing individually, try to combine them. It looks easy, but sometimes things are harder than they look, so take it slow!

Example 3b

Now let's try the exact same thing, but on an A Major chord.

Example 3c

Next, try it on B7. Don't forget that, this time, the second finger of the fretting hand moves between the fifth and sixth strings to play the boom chick bassline.

Example 3d

The next stage is to combine the three chords into a short progression. Obviously, there's a lot happening with the chord changes, the basslines and the added finger picks, so it's easy to lose focus and control of the music. The secret is to begin slowly enough that you can perform the chord changes without leaving any rhythmic gaps between the chords. Everything needs to be smooth and in time, with no hesitation at all.

At this stage, it's important to see yourself as *programming* the muscle memory in your picking hand. If you go slowly, you will program your hand correctly and it'll be easy to speed up and play more complex ideas. However, if you try to run before you can walk, you'll program your hand inaccurately and run into difficulty quite quickly.

When I was younger, I was given the erroneous advice that it's the drummer's job to keep time, which meant the rest of the band felt free to have bad time! It's not the drummer's job to keep time, it's *everyone's* job to keep time. One of the best things I ever did was to begin working with a metronome and I advise you to do the same. At first, I felt imprisoned by it and couldn't get things sounding "in the pocket", but I quickly got used to it and it set me free.

Get used to using a metronome in your practice times and become *aware* of how you are playing over the pulse. Playing in time takes a while to master, but it's an essential part of your musical arsenal.

Play through the following exercise slowly and smoothly. Make sure you can play it five times through with no mistakes before trying to speed it up. Begin with your metronome set to 50bpm.

Example 3e

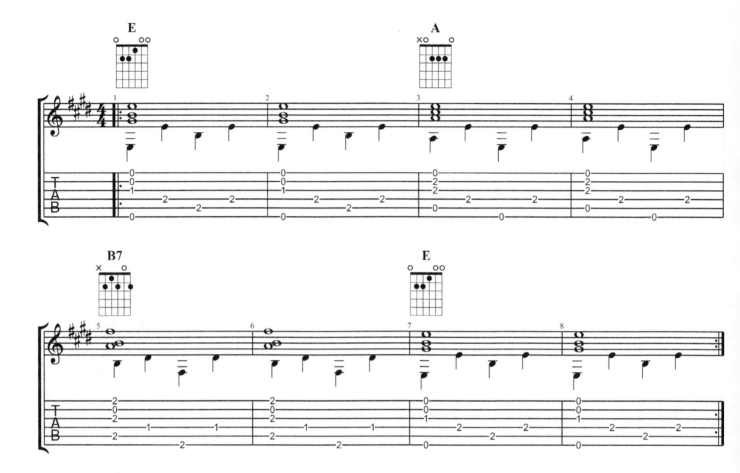

When you've developed some confidence with the previous exercise, try it again, but now think more about your picking hand position. See if you can rest it on the saddle/bridge of your guitar so that the bass notes are slightly muted and the picked chords ring out brightly.

The following exercise teaches you to combine C Major, F Major and G Major with boom chick picking and the chords on beat one. Use either a full barre for the F Major or hook your thumb over the neck like me.

Example 3f

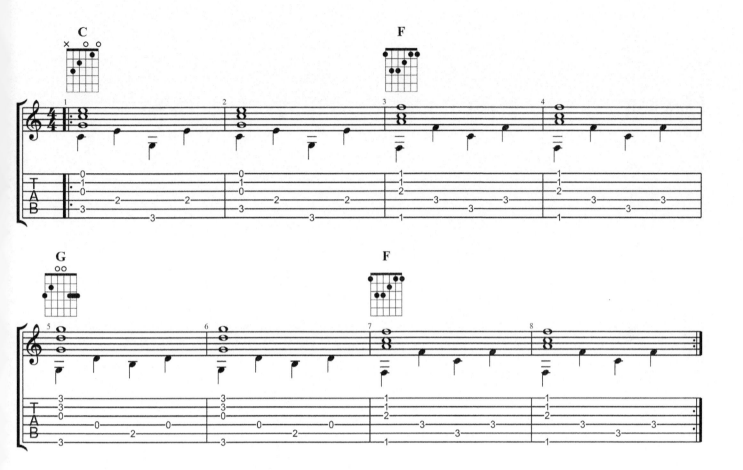

Again, begin slowly and make sure every note is accurate before you speed up. Listen to the sound of the bass notes. Are they muted? Are the high notes ringing out clearly?

The next example combines the chords of A Major, D Major and E Major.

Example 3g

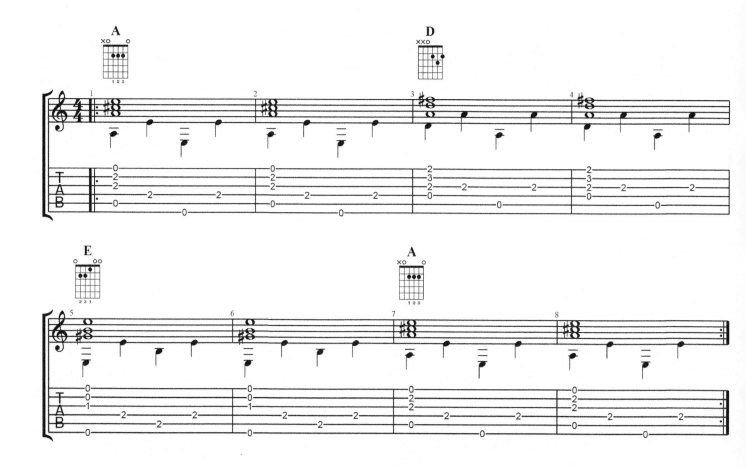

Earlier, you learnt that you can play D Major with an F# in the bass. Repeat the previous example and use the D/F# chord instead of D Major.

Finally, let's try these ideas with barre chords. Experiment by using traditional barre chords as well as my technique of hooking the thumb over the neck to play the bass notes.

Example 3h

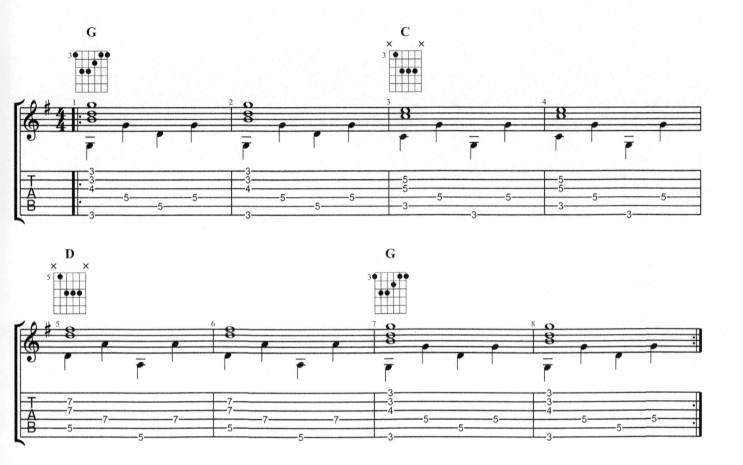

Example 3i reintroduces the C shape barre chord to play the E chord. Watch out for the bassline alternating between 0 and 7 on the low E string.

Example 3i

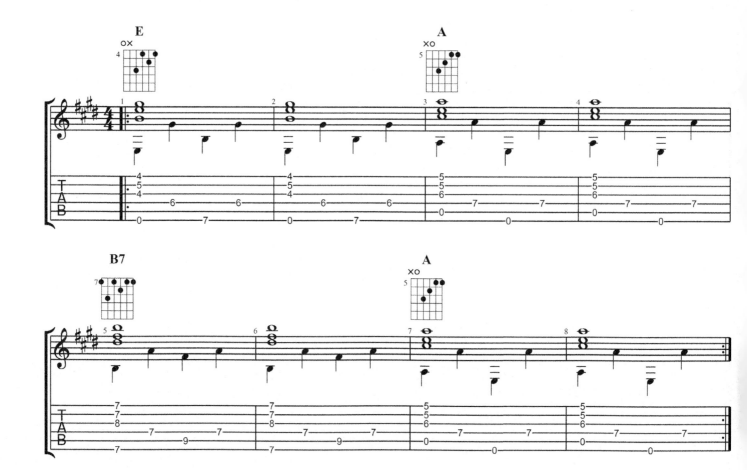

Syncopated chords

Now it's time to add a little more interest to the rhythm of the chord part, while keeping the boom chick bass part perfectly in time.

In music, we don't just count "1 2 3 4" to stay in time, we often split the beat in half and count "1 and 2 and 3 and 4 and…"

The numbers are counted at the same speed as the first "1 2 3 4" and the "ands" are squeezed in between.

First, let's learn the new rhythm. You're going to play a three-fingered chord on beat one, and on the second half of beat two. I'll highlight in bold the beats where you need to pluck the strings. The rhythm goes…

"**One** and two and three **and** four and **one** and two and three **and** four and…"

If you're unsure about this, listen to the audio track that you can download from **www.fundamental-changes. com** and copy the sound.

Playing chords or melodies on the *offbeat* like this is called *syncopation*. Play with a metronome at first, to get the chord sounding on the right beats.

Example 3j

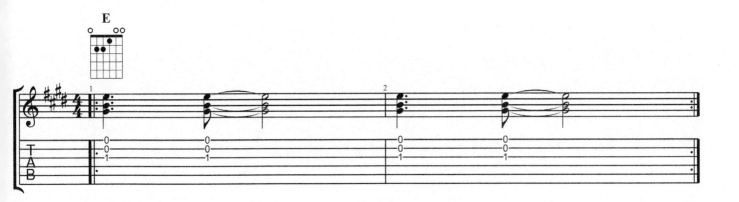

Now we can add in the boom chick bass. This is where we truly start to build independence between the fingers and thumb and open the door to playing more intricate fingerstyle guitar. However, this is also where things may start to get a bit more difficult.

This is important: the straight, boom chick rhythm of the thumb needs to happen *completely independently* of the syncopated chords in the fingers.

It may feel like you're rubbing your tummy and patting your head at first, but please persevere. Once you've broken the back of this exercise, everything will begin to get easier.

This is one of the most important exercises in the whole book, so take your time and make sure that your playing lines up perfectly with the audio track.

A quick word of warning…

Something that I spot with many of my students is the tendency to add an extra chord pluck at the end of the bar. Often, they don't even know they're doing it! Be disciplined and make sure that you're only playing two chord strikes per bar.

Example 3k

Now you're getting the hang of that, let's start moving the rhythm between two chords, E Major and A Major.

Example 3l

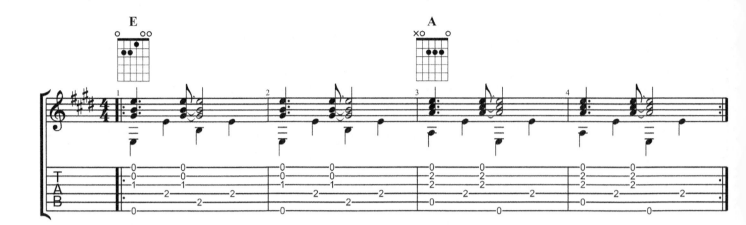

Before we add the B7 chord into the sequence, practice it in isolation. It's one of the more challenging syncopations to master. Remember, you need to move your second finger across the strings to keep the alternating bassline going while playing the chord stabs.

Example 3m

When you're confident with the B7, add it into the full progression.

I can't stress enough how important it is to go slowly with these exercises. Imagine you're programming a robot. It's much easier to get it right the first time, rather than have to unlearn the movement and reprogram your hand later.

Example 3n

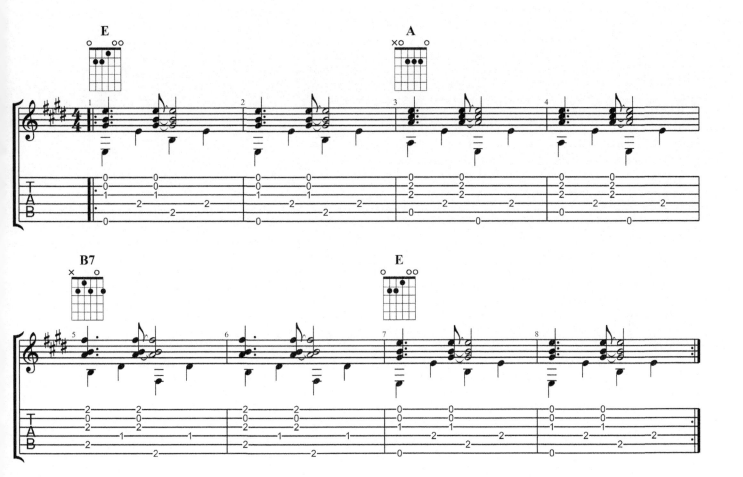

When you can play the previous example perfectly four times in a row at 60 bpm, allow yourself to start increasing the metronome speed bit by bit.

Let's try the same exercise with some different chords. Here it is with C Major, F Major and G Major.

Example 3o

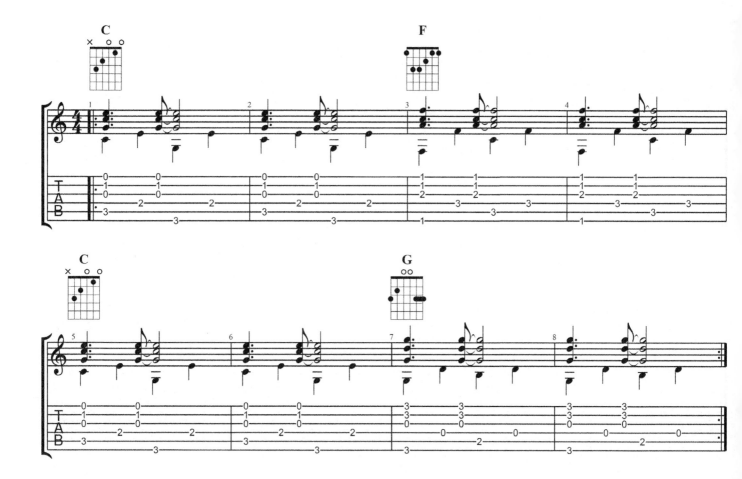

Now try the same exercise with barre chords.

Example 3p

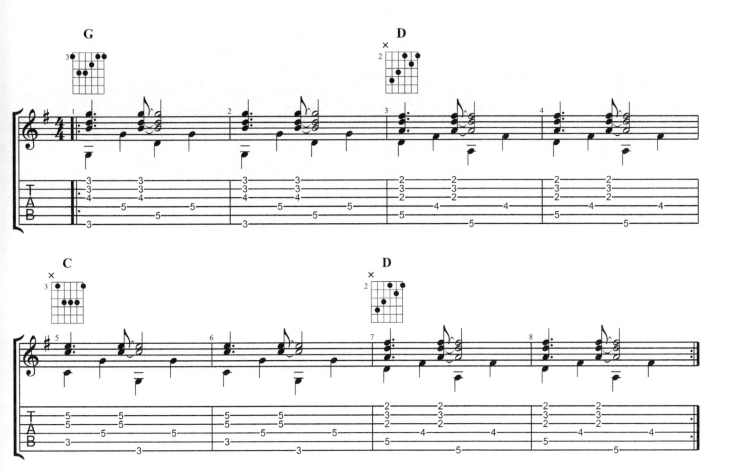

We've been using similar chord sequences for all the exercises so far, so here are a few more chords you should know. Play them with the written alternating basslines, using both the one-chord-per-bar pattern and the syncopated chord pattern too.

Example 3q

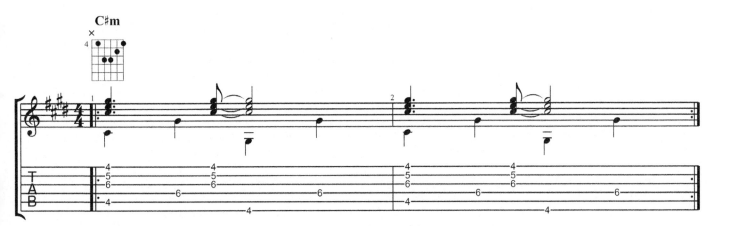

Example 3r

Now you've got a few more chord shapes in your arsenal, we can incorporate these colors into longer musical progressions. Play each of the following three sequences, first with one chord per bar and, when you can play that cleanly, move on to playing the syncopated rhythm.

Example 3s

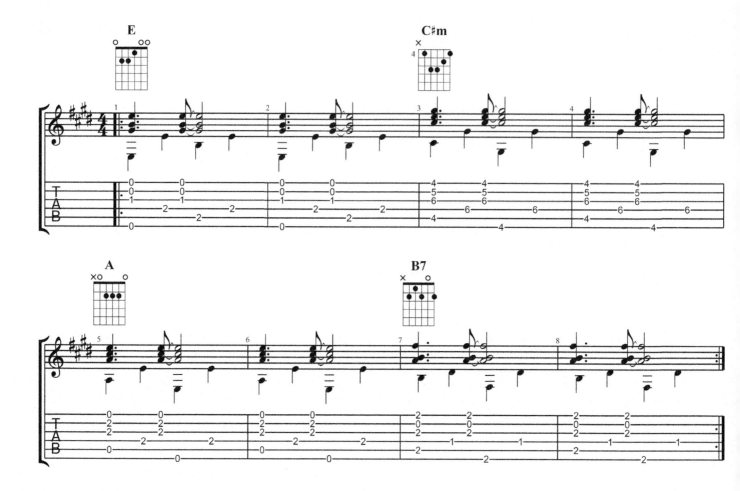

Example 3t

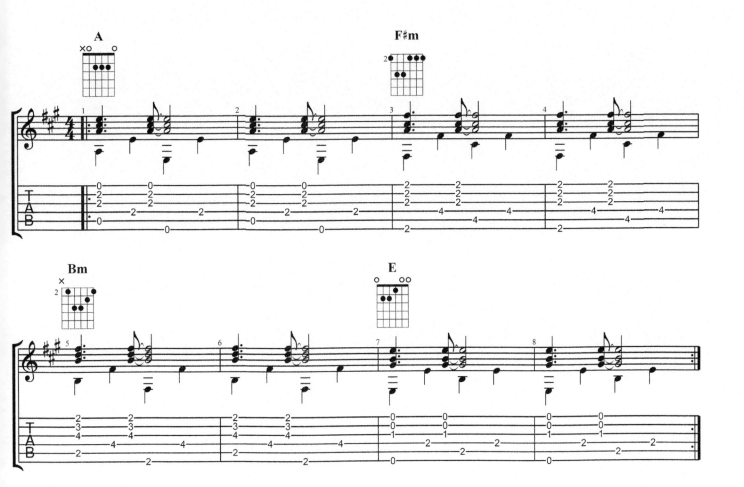

Example 3u

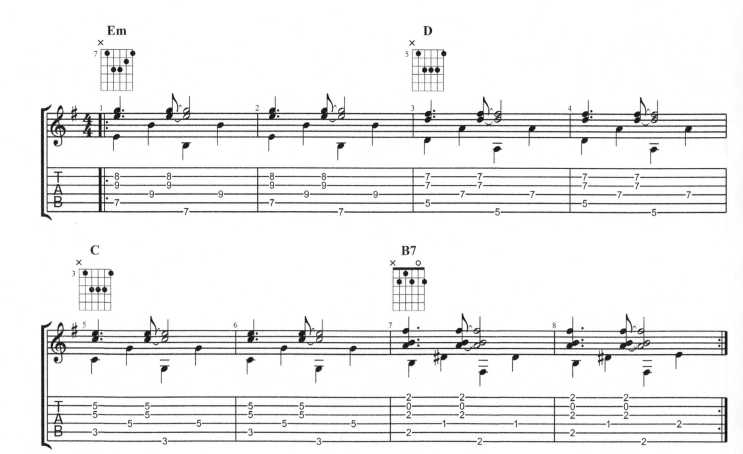

Example 3v

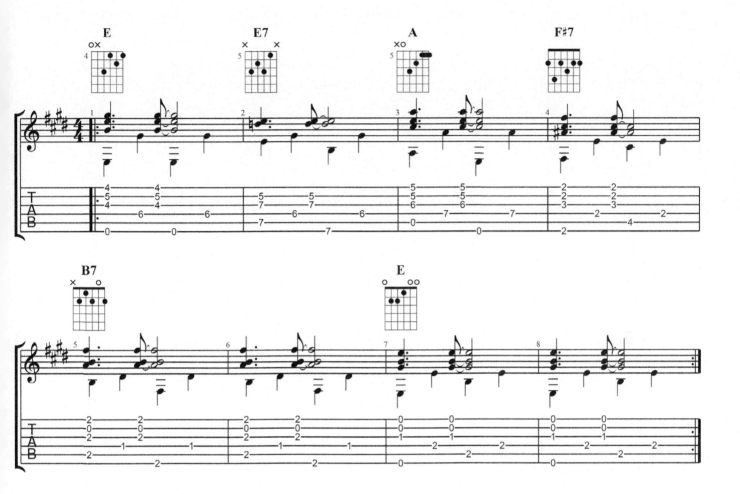

Playing these exercises with the one-chord-per-bar pattern really forces you to speed up the changes, and it trains both hands to work together much more tightly. Make sure you apply it to all the exercises in this chapter.

Here is one more piece of advice I'd like to pass on: the most important thing for me, when I play this style of music, is making the melody *feel* and *sound* good. When I learn a song, I work out an arrangement then practice it. Once I've practiced it enough so that my hands know what they are doing, I'll focus on making the melody feel good. Sometimes, if I'm playing a single line melody with my thumbpick, in order to bring out different dynamics and tones I will turn the thumbpick on a slight angle. Making small adjustments like this help to produce a range of tones and bring out that voice-like quality of the instrument.

We've done lots more groundwork in this chapter, and now it's over to you! I'd like you to apply this syncopated rhythm to any chord sequences you know in any key. You can pick any song you like and add the rhythms in this chapter. The most important thing is to keep working on the independence between the boom chick bassline and chord stabs.

Chapter Four: Arpeggios and Finger Picking

In the previous chapter, you learned how to combine the boom chick picking pattern with plucked chords played both on the beat and syncopated against a steady bassline.

In this section, you'll discover how to develop independence in your picking fingers and play more intricate melodies. Here we are going to build much more control between your fingers and your thumb.

Let's begin to train your picking fingers with some exercises that will lock in the patterns you need to know.

First, we'll teach your picking fingers to pick through the top three strings of the E Major chord while your thumb plays the boom chick rhythm on the bass strings.

Let's begin by separating out the melody part before we add the bass. Hold down an E Major chord and use your index finger to play the G string, your middle finger to play the B string, and your ring finger to play the high E string.

Example 4a

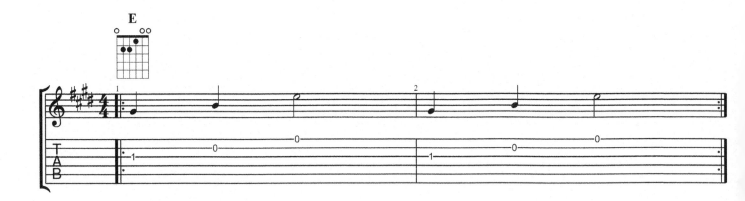

When you've got the hang of that, let's add the boom chick back in. This is a critical exercise. To begin with you may find yourself flailing around like a beginner! Don't worry, because everyone is the same. I can only do this so cleanly because I spent hours and hours of practice working on it.

I can't stress it enough – go slowly and make sure each note is correct. Try to hear the melody and bass as completely separate parts. This will help you to isolate and internalize them.

Example 4b

The example above will take some time to master. I've taught this exercise to some very accomplished guitarists and they all said it was like they'd never picked up the guitar before. However, with some focused practice for 15 minutes, they all started to get to grips with it, and after a few hours they were quite proficient.

I've drilled this exercise so much that when I look down at my picking hand I feel like, "Oh! What's going on there?!" It looks crazy to me, because after so many hours in the woodshed, it's all completely unconscious and happens by feel.

The point is, you need to be patient and dedicated if you want to succeed.

Start the exercise without a metronome and, to begin with, just make sure that every pick is correct. When you can play it evenly, add a metronome at around 50bpm and gradually build up the speed to 120bpm.

Try the same pattern on an A Major chord.

Example 4c

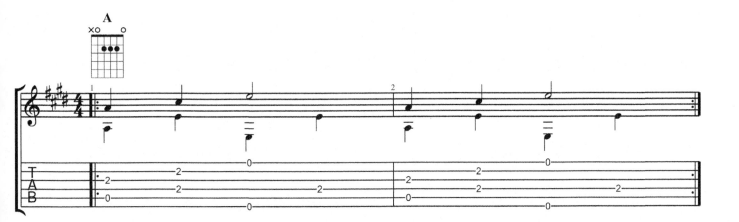

Make sure you're solid with the previous exercise, as the boom chick pattern is slightly different from the E Major chord.

Now learn how to play this idea with the B7 chord. Don't forget, the second finger of the fretting hand must move between the 5th and 6th strings to take care of the bassline. While this is something you may have been comfortable with before, playing it with the picked arpeggio on the top three strings is a whole different barrel of fish.

When things get a bit more complicated like this, it's a good idea to study the notation carefully and look at your picking hand. Pay attention to which notes are played together at the same time. For example, in the B7 exercise below, you play the 2nd fret bass note on the 6th string *at the same time* as picking the highest note in beat three.

If you can figure out these little "hit points" to target, you will find the coordination of your fingers easier to manage.

Example 4d

Now we've worked through each of the three chords individually, let's stick them together. The following etude is written with two bars per chord, but you may find it useful to double up and play four bars per chord to begin with to lock in the patterns. When you're confident playing four bars of each chord, you can return to playing the exercise as written.

Example 4e

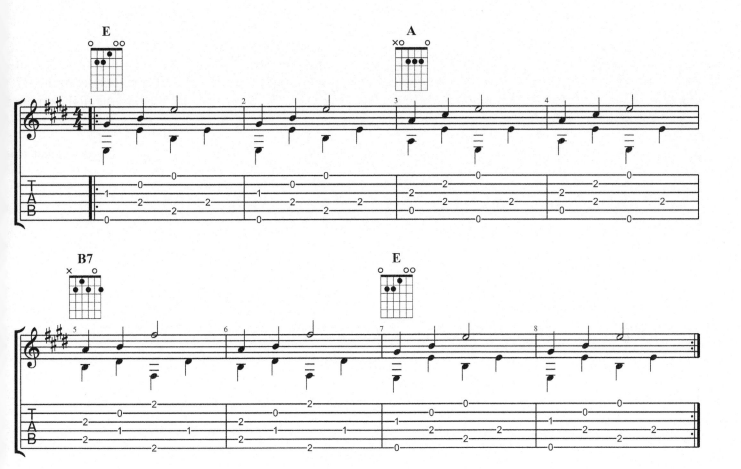

The most difficult part of the previous example is definitely the chord change from B7 back to E Major and it's all too easy to make the music come to a shuddering halt at this point. Let's isolate that change and work on it with a metronome.

Set your metronome to 50bpm and play through the following example. If you can't play it at 50bpm, slow it down until there is no rhythmic break when you change between the two chords. Repeat the following example four times in a row with no break.

Example 4f

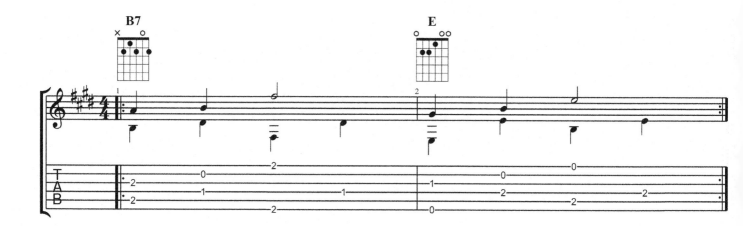

As you gain confidence and the picking becomes more natural, increase the metronome speed by 8bpm and play four more times through the exercise. Keep repeating this process until you reach 120 bpm. Yes, it's a lot of work, but do it once and do it right and you'll have programmed your muscle memory forever.

Now, we're going to add in a short *double time* section to the B7 to help develop more overall control of your playing. Set your metronome to 60bpm and play normal 1/4 notes for three bars before playing the fourth bar as 1/8th notes (twice as quick). Loop this exercise, playing one double-time bar out of every four.

This is a great exercise you can use anytime, whenever you're having difficulty speeding up your picking.

Example 4g

Moving forward, it's time to apply these picked arpeggio ideas to progressions in different keys. First, let's begin with A Major.

Example 4h

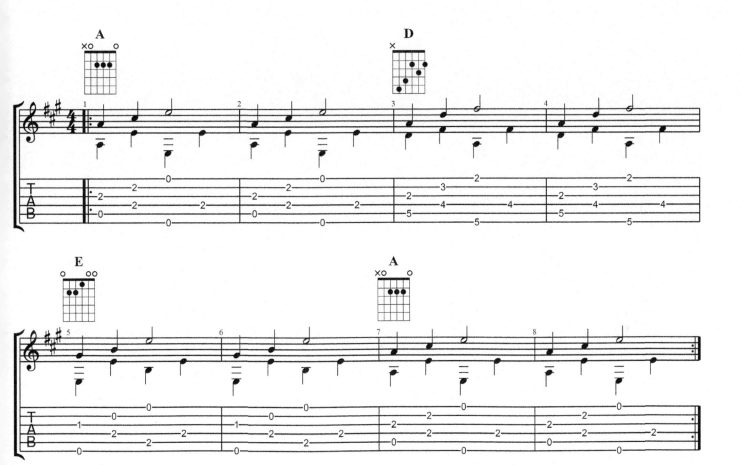

Now try it in G Major.

Example 4i

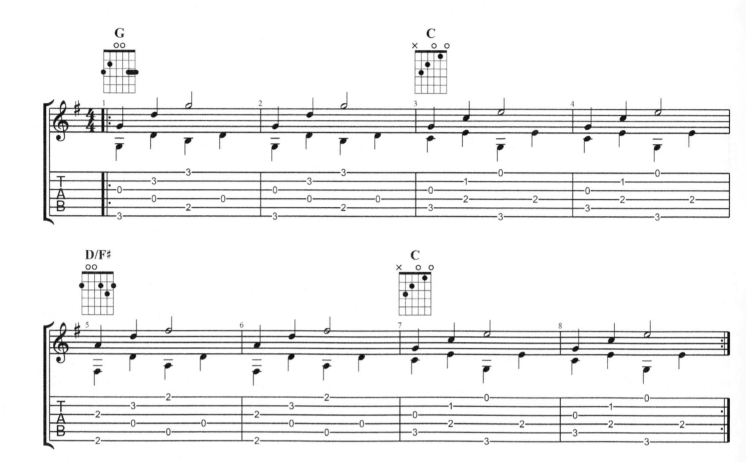

Let's see how this arpeggio-based picking pattern is affected when you play barre chords. Try it with a C-shape E Major chord to begin with.

There are two ways to play the bass pattern. First, you can use the open E string without moving your pinkie.

Example 4j

The other way is to move your little finger across the strings to play the 7th fret, as you've done before.

Example 4k

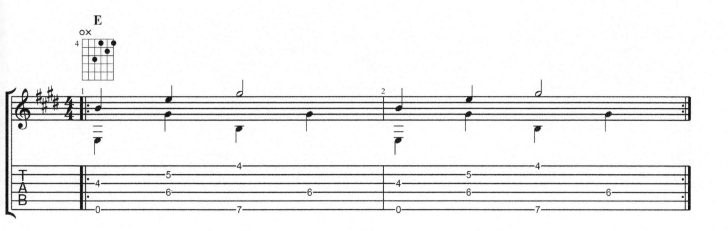

The above two examples have slightly different sounds and can be used as you feel appropriate. Pick one to begin with and stick with it for now.

Now move the C-shape barre chord down to the 5th fret to play a D Major chord. In this position you can use the open fifth string to play the final bass note in the boom chick rhythm and avoid playing the sixth string altogether.

Example 4l

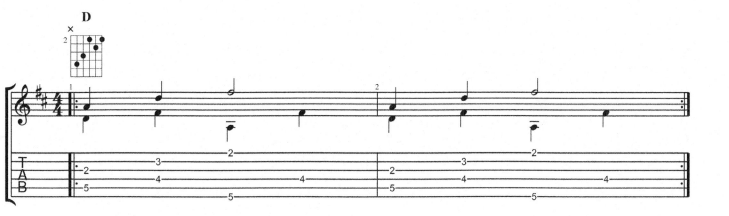

To tie the previous ideas together, try this progression in the key of G. Pay attention to where I play the chords.

Example 4m

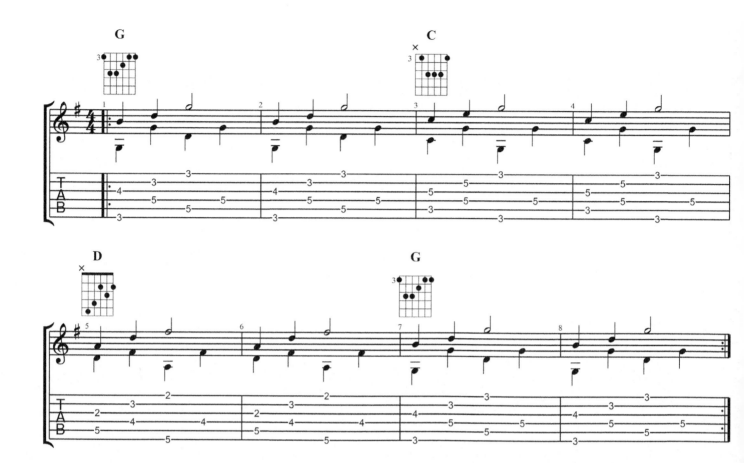

Phew! That was a tricky example, but go slow and you'll pick it up with a bit of patience.

Before we move on, repeat the previous examples and play them all with just one bar per chord instead of two. That'll give you a good picking workout!

We're now keeping the boom chick rhythm alive and steady with the thumb and adding some beautiful arpeggio ideas with the picking fingers. However, there's plenty more you can do with those fingers. After all the work we've done in this chapter, the following idea might fry your brain a little, but go slowly and you'll open up a whole world of possibilities.

The idea is simple: *reverse the direction of the picking fingers.*

Instead of picking the 3rd, 2nd then 1st string, we're going to pick the 1st, 2nd then 3rd. It's harder than it sounds, especially after all the programming you've done.

When I learnt to do this, I could literally feel the pathways in my brain developing! Go slow and remember to look for those hit points where your fingers and thumb come together. They'll help to keep you steady.

Let's begin with the E Major chord.

Example 4n

I won't waste space by writing out this picking pattern for the whole chord progression we've been working on, because you know the drill by now. Here's a summary of what you need to do:

- Practice it on both the A Major and B7 chords

- Then combine them with the E Major to build the E Major – A Major – B7 – E Major sequence we've been using as a workhorse

- Start with two bars per chord, develop your speed and control, then slow down and switch to playing one bar per chord before increasing the speed gradually

- When you're confident with the sequence above, play it in the keys of A Major and C Major

- Finally, use the picking pattern on the longer progressions we played earlier

Now, there are two more 1/4 note picking patterns you should know.

The first is to play the 2nd string, 3rd string then the 1st string with the fingers. Here's that pattern on an E Major chord.

Example 4o

When you have got to grips with this pattern, apply it to all the other chords we've covered and use it in the chord sequences.

Next, learn the following idea that uses the sequence 3rd string, 1st string, 2nd string.

Example 4p

Again, apply this pattern to every chord and progression we've covered so far.

If you want to be methodical, you can work through the fingerpicking permutations I've *not* covered above. They're easy to figure out on paper and there are six possibilities. I'll list the order in which you can play the top three strings here to give you a starting point. The two you've not studied are written in italics.

123, *132, 213*, 231, 312, 321

Of course, this list doesn't include patterns where the same string is played twice, but once you've got to grips with the ideas above, you'll find that it's much easier to deal with whatever is put in front of you.

The finger picking patterns in this chapter are just the start of your journey. I'll say it one more time, you must learn everything slowly and carefully otherwise you'll quickly fall at the next hurdle. The goal is to make the picking hand movement completely internalized and unconscious, so you can focus on playing great melodies and chords with your fretting hand.

Congratulations! You've come a long way. In the next chapter we're going to take a look at some more advanced picking patterns that build on the great work you've done here. Only move on when you feel you're ready.

Chapter Five: Advanced Picking Patterns

Welcome back Thrill Seekers!

So far, we have built some independence between our thumb and fingers, learnt some chords, discovered how to play a bassline, and added some groovy fingerpicking ideas. Now it's time to build on those successes and develop even more control in your picking hand.

In this section, we're going to discover some more intricate picking patterns, build some speed, and explore syncopation a little further.

Our starting point is syncopation.

As you learnt earlier, not all music is played on the beat – in fact, it would be very boring if it was! Often, melody notes are played between the beats and whole phrases seem to float across the pulse of the song. If you're going to play interesting tunes, or anything with a swing feel, you need to learn to place the melody notes between the beats using your picking fingers, all while keeping a steady boom chick going with your thumb.

The best way to begin is to take a picking pattern you already know and alter it slightly to *anticipate* some of the notes. I'll show you what I mean.

Refresh your memory by taking another look at the picked arpeggio pattern on the beat.

Now we will *anticipate* the final two picked notes in bar two by an 1/8th note. This means we will play *half a beat earlier* while the thumb keeps its strict boom chick rhythm. This is a bit tougher than it sounds, so listen to the audio and play through this example carefully.

Example 5a

At first, the natural tendency of your thumb is to try and synchronize with the picking fingers and copy what they're doing. It's very important that you watch out for this and keep the thumb moving in 1/4 notes on the beat. If you find this happening, play through the exercise one note at a time, very slowly, and focus on how the final two melody notes fall *in between* each thumb strike.

Learn how to play this two-bar pattern on the chords of E Major, A Major and B7 before combining them into the following sequence.

Example 5b

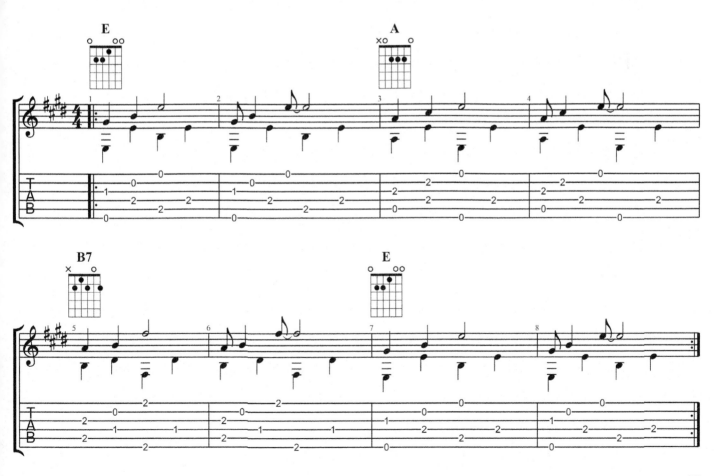

Make sure you can play this pattern on all the chord sequences we've covered so far.

The next stage in your fingerstyle development is to isolate and play *only* the anticipated rhythm in bar two. In other words, we'll play two bars of the syncopated rhythm without playing the "straight" version first. You'll find this takes a little more concentration but it's great for your picking control.

Example 5c

Apply this picking pattern to all the chords and progressions you know during your practice sessions. When you're ready, play just one bar on each chord.

Moving on, let's repeat the syncopated rhythm but reverse the direction of the arpeggio.

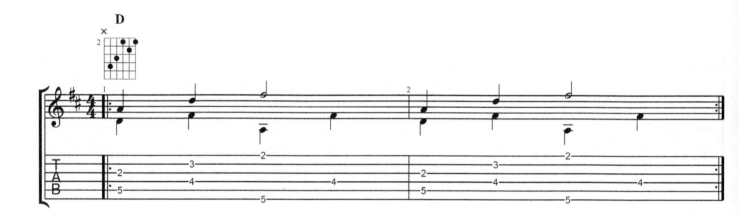

Now we'll switch chords and try that again, anticipating the melody in bar two.

Example 5d

As always, learn this rhythm on E Major, A Major and B7, then combine these chords to create the short sequence we've been working with. When you can play that sequence, transfer the full two-bar pattern to all the other progressions we've covered.

As your confidence with this pattern builds, use only the syncopated second bar on each progression, and eventually you will be playing short etudes like this one in the key of C Major.

Example 5e

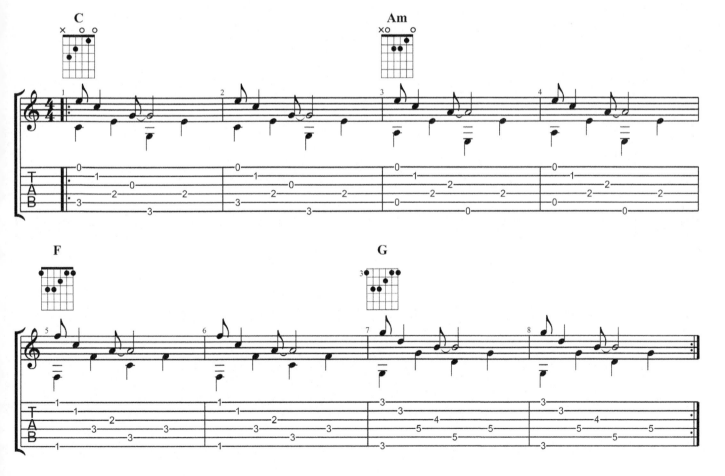

Finally, reduce the amount of time spent on each chord to just one bar to help develop the coordination between both hands.

Example 5f

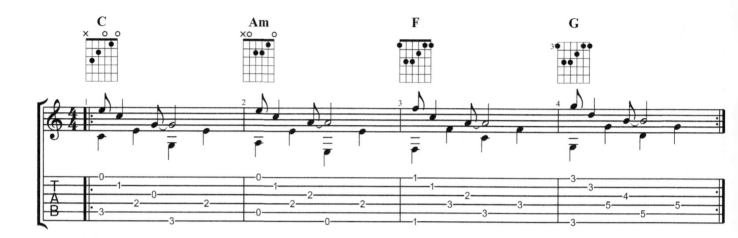

Watch out for any trouble spots and slow down if there's any break in rhythm when you change chords. For example, the jump from the G Major barre chord back to C Major may cause a few issues to begin with. Slow down your metronome until you find a speed where you can play the exercise smoothly and gradually speed up from there.

Of course, we can syncopate any of the fingerpicking permutations we've covered. To save space, I'm only going to notate the first two bars of the patterns. I'll leave you to work through the steps to apply them to all chords and progressions and reduce them to one-bar phrases.

Example 5g

Example 5h

Example 5i

Example 5j

These exercises are developing more independence between your thumb and fingers. Now you are getting used to syncopated patterns, let's have some fun by adding a bit of speed to your picking hand!

The quickest way to build up speed is to squeeze an extra note into a picking pattern that you already know. Let's use our workhorse pattern to get started.

All we will do to begin with is add an extra pick on the 3rd string between beats two and three.

Example 5k

Gradually speed up Example 5k with a metronome before moving on. Aim to reach 120bpm. As always, apply this picking pattern to other chords and progressions.

As you can hear, even adding just one extra pick makes a huge difference to the sound of the music, but we don't have to stop there. Let's add a couple more notes.

Example 5l

Again, speed up this example and apply it to all your other chords.

Now return to the earlier list of 1/4 note picking permutations and try adding faster notes in wherever you feel appropriate. Remember, the string permutations are 123, 132, 213, 231, 312, 321. Begin by adding just one extra pick and gradually try to fill up the bar.

You won't use busy picking patterns like this all the time, but they are great for developing creative ideas and increasing the dexterity of the picking hand.

A great way to create interesting and unique fingerpicking patterns is to combine one bar of a faster pattern with one bar of a syncopated one, like this.

Example 5m

I'm sure you're starting to realize that you can have a lot of fun playing with these ideas and the sky really is the limit! Apply everything you do to all the chord sequences you know and work with a metronome until you can play everything fast and clean.

If you get stuck for ideas, you can return to the permutations above and build from there. But how about going back to the master? Listen to some Chet Atkins songs and try to copy his picking patterns. You'll learn a great deal very quickly.

That's enough exercises for now. Let's move on and discover how we can add melody to our music and play some songs – all with the boom chick bassline.

Chapter Six: Pre-Song Exercises

We're just one step away from learning some great songs. Before you dive into this chapter, make sure you're confident with everything we've covered so far.

In this section, we're going to work through a set of melodic exercises that will help you build the skills and coordination needed to combine chords, melody and bass musically. Here you'll learn a few techniques that you'll need to play the songs that follow. First up is the *hammer-on*.

A hammer-on is created by a fretting finger hammering onto the fretboard to sound a note. You can hammer on from one fretted note to another, or by picking an open string then hammering onto a fretted note.

Begin by learning this short sequence of hammer-ons based around an Am chord. Notice how the first note is played before the first beat and the hammer-on note lands on beat one.

Example 6a

If you've never played a hammer-on before, you may find this exercise quite challenging. You can develop your technique by picking the sequence of notes first, before gradually introducing hammer-ons.

It's important to use the tips of your fingers to hammer the notes, otherwise you'll accidently hit adjacent strings or prevent the note from sounding properly.

Let's focus on the first two notes of the previous exercise and gradually reintroduce the boom chick bassline.

Since the first note of the melody is played just before the start of the bar (on beat 4&), it's the second note of the melody that's played on the beat. Remember our rule, that the root note is always played on beat one? This means that the second note of the phrase is hammered on at *exactly* the same time as the open A bass note is picked. This might sound obvious, but when you're first starting out, perfectly syncing a picked bass note with a melody note that is hammered on is deceptively challenging.

Here's a very short exercise that will help develop this skill.

The idea is to pick the open 3rd string, then hammer on to the second fret and pick the open A string simultaneously. To begin with, hammer on with whichever finger feels strongest. That'll probably be your second finger.

Example 6b

When you've managed to sync the hammer-on and the picked bass note, repeat Exercise 6b using your third finger to perform the hammer-on.

When that's feeling nice and strong, repeat Exercise 6b, but this time hammer your second finger onto the 2nd fret of the fourth string, as if playing the bottom note of the Am chord. You may hear some of the lower note sound, but make sure that the hammer-on on the third string is the strongest note.

Example 6c

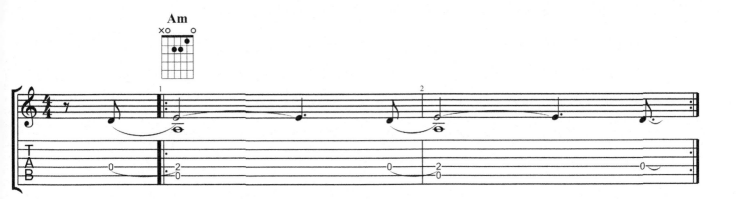

The next stage is to expand the melody to include notes on the second string. Be careful though, only pick the first note on the second string and hammer onto the 1st fret with your first finger.

Example 6d

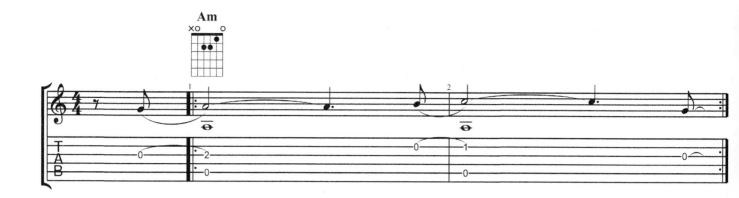

When you've developed a nice, strong hammer-on to the 1st fret, it's time to add in the rest of the boom chick bass pattern. Go slowly, as it's easy to lose the rhythm when you're trying to coordinate the picked bass notes and hammered melody notes.

Example 6e

The previous exercise is quite a challenge for most people when they're first starting out. There's a lot going on and if you've never played a hammer-on before you might need to do a bit of separate study.

Most guitarists will fumble with the previous exercise for quite a while and it's common to lose volume in the melody part or accidentally pick too many notes that should be hammered. This should encourage you, because you're not alone! Do persevere, because this exercise is great training for your independence, and it'll teach your brain some new tricks.

The next thing we're going to do is to bolt on a couple of extra notes to the melody. I want you to add the hammered melody line on the B string and finish the phrase on the open E string. It's written below with the bassline, but you should isolate the melody and learn to play that first.

It will help to pick each note to begin with, but as soon as you can play it, go back to hammer-ons, as you're only allowed to pick the first note on each string!

When you're ready, and you're getting smooth hammer-ons with good volume, add the bassline back in. You may find it helps to loop Example 6e a few times before you extend the melody to include the notes below.

Example 6f

As your confidence with the previous exercise builds, do a quick check to ensure that all the musical components are in place:

- You should be muting the bass strings with the heel of your picking hand

- You should be playing a rock-solid bassline

- The melody should be strong and ring out

- Everything should feel unconscious and natural

Here are a few more legato melodies to learn over different chords. Remember, only pick the first note on each chord. Break these examples down and learn them just as you did with the A Minor melody.

Example 6g

Example 6h

Example 6i

Just like learning songs, you now need to begin to learn these melodies and basslines as single units, beat by beat. When playing embellished passages like these, we can no longer separate the parts, learn them individually, then combine them like we did at the very beginning. That was fine when we were playing very simple patterns, but now the whole passage needs to be learnt as one, which means going very slowly and focusing on every single movement that occurs on every single beat.

We've looked at playing some ascending melodies with hammer-ons, now let's look at some descending melodies that use pull-offs.

As you may have guessed, a pull-off is the opposite of a hammer-on, and is played by pulling your finger downwards off a higher fretted note to a lower one. The lower note can either be fretted or be an open string.

Place your second finger on the 2nd fret of the 3rd string. Pick the note and then smoothly pull your finger off the string in the direction of the floor. If you've done it right, you should hear how the fretting finger "plucks" the string, just like a pick.

Example 6j

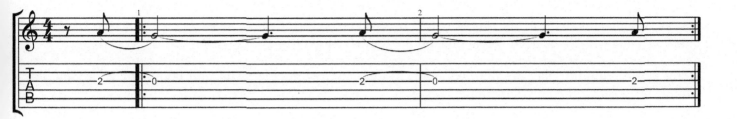

Learn this melody based around an A Minor chord.

Example 6k

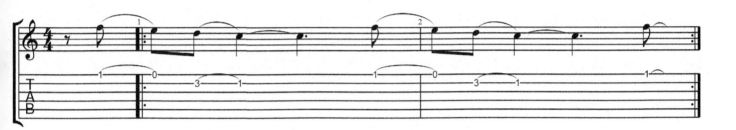

As with the hammer-on exercises, the first note of the melody is played just before the start of the bar (on beat 4&), so it's the second note that syncs with the first thumbed bass note on the A string. We must pull off to the second note of the phrase precisely as the thumb hits the fifth string. Believe me, this is quite difficult and will probably require lots of practice.

In the following example, pick the first note (F) then pull-off to the open E string. Play the first bass note on the open A string with your thumb, simultaneously with the open high E string. If you like, you can use your second finger to hold down the 2nd fret on the fourth string, even though you won't use it in this example.

Example 6l

The previous idea looks simple on paper, but it is deceptively difficult to play. Have patience and only move forward when you can play both melody notes cleanly and with equal volume.

The next example uses the E note on the 2nd fret, fourth string. You'll notice that it's part of the A Minor chord and the second note in the boom chick rhythm. Did you notice that I haven't asked you to hold the *full* A Minor chord? Right now, all we need is that note on the fourth string.

Here, you're going to play the first two notes of the melody and add in the full boom chick bassline for A Minor. Make sure you always use a pull-off in the melody. It's easy to forget and pick both notes.

Example 6m

When you've got to grips with that, let's add in the final two notes of the melody. You'll find the pull-off on the second string quite challenging to begin with. It's easy to lose volume when you pull off with your fourth finger, but stick with it and it'll gradually get stronger. Practice the pull-off in isolation if you need to, before adding it back into the full phrase.

Example 6n

Finally, to push you a bit further, here's a simple way to extend the A Minor melody.

Example 6o

These examples are tough because syncing a hammer-on or pull-off with a picked note on a different string is an unusual movement for most players. However, these movements are a fundamental part of fingerstyle guitar playing, so you need to get used to them. I promise you they get easier, but you may need to do some isolated hammer-on and pull-off technique practice to develop these skills independently, especially if you're just starting out.

The following few ideas will help you to build finger independence with pull-off melodies on different chords. As with everything in this book, explore your own ideas, make them your own and have fun. Once you've broken the back of this important technique, you'll find that everything you do in the future is much easier.

Example 6p

Example 6q

Example 6r

We made it! Congratulations on working through this difficult section. The exercises here may take you hours, days, or even weeks to master, but whatever your timescale, don't worry! I know you're anxious to get playing some songs, but they'll be much easier to tackle once you get these fundamental techniques mastered. Take these exercises seriously, but enjoy taking your time to get these important skills down.

When you're ready, let's move on and put all this preparation into practice. It's time to learn some songs!

Chapter Seven: Learning Songs

Let's take a moment to appreciate how far you've come.

- You started by playing a simple boom chick bassline with your thumb, then you added chords and played them on and off the beat

- Next, you developed your fingerpicking with arpeggios and learnt to syncopate them

- Then you discovered how to play more advanced patterns, while building speed and complexity

- In the previous chapter, you learnt the legato techniques used to add melody to chords and synced everything to that all-important boom chick bassline

You've really come a long way and you should be proud of your progress. If there's anything you're not 100% sure about, go back and get it solid before diving into this chapter. You're going to need to be firing on all cylinders!

In this chapter, we're going to combine all the skills you've learnt into some fun songs. In time, when you've mastered these short arrangements, you'll have a huge sense of accomplishment and you'll have some great pieces to play for friends and family, and with other musicians.

First, however, I want to pass on some advice on how to go about learning songs. This is what has always worked for me over many years as a guitarist.

First of all, go very slowly and memorize *everything* – every note, every phrase, every position on the guitar.

Next, remember that now you are handling more difficult arrangements, you can't learn the bassline and melody individually, then combine them. Instead, you need to learn them together, note by note, bar by bar, and understand how they interact.

I don't read music, so I've always learnt everything by ear. I learn songs by memorizing them. I start off learning things note by note, then piece together phrases and sections until it all joins up. This is a great way to learn as it's thorough and meticulous. It teaches you to play *music* and know that every part of the song is correct. Even if you're a great reader, I encourage you to memorize these tunes, so that you're thinking less about the dots and more about the music.

Learning through repetition means that you can forget about the mechanics of playing the piece, focus purely on the music, and really get inside it. When everything comes together as a cohesive whole, those are the moments we live for as musicians.

The Beginner's Blues

The first song you'll learn is *The Beginner's Blues*. I wrote this especially for you because I wanted to teach you something that was fun, achievable, but still a little bit challenging. It combines the boom chick bassline with chords you've already covered in the key of E Major, but adds a legato melody and some syncopation.

As you'll hear on the audio download, this track has a swing groove, but as you work through it, I suggest you play each section straight to begin with, to get the mechanics right, then add the swing later. Also, you may wish to begin by picking every melody note with your fingers before adding the pull-offs later.

Here are some further tips:

Bars 1-2:

Hold down the E Major chord and make sure you are comfortable playing the boom chick rhythm. Next, add the hammer-on to the first beat of the bar, from the open third string to the 1st fret. This is a very common movement in blues and country music.

When you can play the third-string hammer-on, stop playing it and go back to playing the boom chick on the E Major chord. It's time to learn the main melody part on the top two strings. The important thing to focus on is where the bassline aligns with the melody note. Notice that the boom chick bass note always synchronizes with an open string in the melody on the first two beats. As with the legato exercises we went through, the pull-off to an open string occurs exactly as you pick the bass note with your thumb. Make sure that the bass note is plucked just as the open string sounds.

When you can play the boom chick rhythm with the melody, reintroduce the initial hammer-on and start to add some swing.

Bars 3-4:

The melody is repeated over an A7 chord before repeating the E Major bar.

Bar 5:

This is the beginning of the turnaround, played over a B7 chord. The only new movement is a little slide from the 2nd to the 3rd fret on the first string, played with the little finger. Notice that I stop playing the boom chick rhythm here and only play the F# in the bass.

Bar 6:

This is a common turnaround lick you should know. It begins at the fifth fret on the fifth string and the whole shape moves down in semitones back to E Major.

Now, work through the tab/notation and see how you get on.

Example 7a – The Beginner's Blues

Buffalo Gals

Buffalo Gals is a country style cowboy campfire song, written by John Hodges in 1844. The song was used in the 1943 Bing Crosby film *Dixie* and is featured prominently in the 1948 movie *It's a Wonderful Life*. *Buffalo Gals* is great for developing your fingerpicking and introduces a couple of new techniques that I want to show you before we dive into the full song.

Example 7b below moves between the chords of G Major and D7 (although the D7 is played with an F# in the bass as we saw earlier).

The first thing I want you to notice here is that the boom chick bass has changed slightly. In *Buffalo Gals*, the bass is only played on the sixth and fourth strings – there's no note played on the fifth string.

In Chapter Six, we covered a lot of exercises that taught you how to play a pull-off that began on the off-beat and landed on the beat. In *Buffalo Gals*, this pattern is reversed on the first two notes, so that the higher (fretted) note is played on the beat.

There are four more challenging parts to this exercise. Let's look at them one by one and find the best solutions.

The first is controlling the pull-offs with the fourth and third fingers while holding down the G Major chord. This becomes easier when you realize that you only need hold down the *root note* on the sixth string to play the full G chord.

Next, the transition between G and D7/F# can be tricky. To move from G Major to D7/F#, the easiest way is to slide your second finger (which is playing the bass note) down a fret and add your first finger to play the 1st fret on the second string. You don't need to fret a note on the third string.

The third challenge is using your pinkie finger to play the pull-off from the 3rd to 1st fret on the D7/F#. The problem here is that the pinkie simply feels a little out of position, and the fourth-to-first finger movement is unusual. Don't worry if it feels strange and uncontrolled at first, it will develop with time and repetition.

Finally, the pull-offs here are *pushed* rhythmically (anticipating the beat) to create a highly syncopated feel. I suggest you learn the whole thing straight, then gradually increase the amount of "push". Listen carefully to the audio to see what I mean.

With all that in mind, work through Example 7b very slowly and piece it together, beat by beat.

Example 7b

When you are confident with the previous exercise, you should have very little trouble playing *Buffalo Gals*. The biggest challenge is to keep the melody strings ringing when you change chords in the bass.

Bars 1-2:

Use your second finger to hold down the G bass note. Use your first and second fingers to play the melody on the top strings while your thumb takes care of the bassline.

Bars 3-4:

In bar 3, slide your second finger down one fret to play the root of the D#/F7 chord. Remember, you don't have to hold the note on the 3rd string. Use your fourth and first fingers to play the pull-off on the second string. Bar 4 is similar to bar 2.

Bars 5-8:

These are identical to bars 1-4 with a slight change to the melody in bars 7-8.

Bars 9-10:

In section two, the melody lifts and becomes a descending idea on the first string. Use the fourth and first fingers to play the first two notes and everything should fall into place. Practice picking these notes and using pull-offs where you can, then use whichever you prefer.

Bars 11-12:

On the D7/F#, the melody is similar to the first section, so again you should use your fourth and first fingers for the pull-off.

Bars 13-16:

These four bars are almost a direct repeat of the previous four with a slight change in the melody to finish.

There you have it! A few new techniques and a great song that will quickly develop your playing. Now have a go at the complete piece.

Example 7c – Buffalo Gals

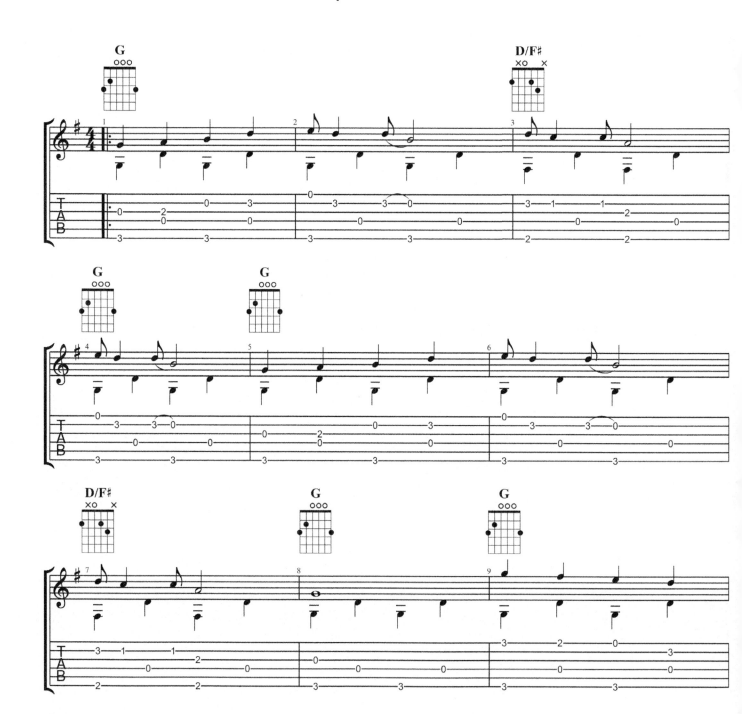

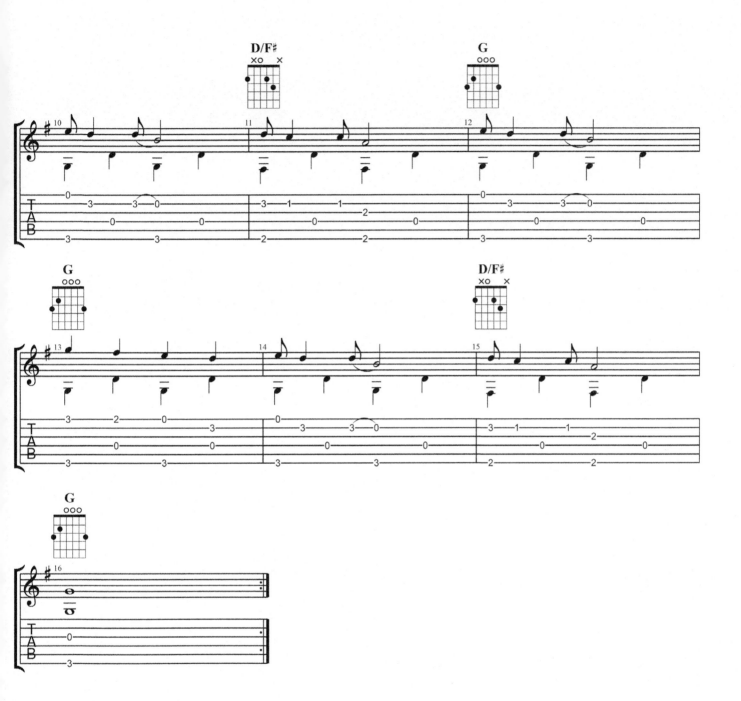

Creole Belle

To finish our fingerstyle journey, I want to leave you with a great little tune called *Creole Belle*. I think the first time I heard it was from the great Doc Watson and I loved it. It's a very simple song, but you can do a lot with it.

While most of us associate *My Creole Belle* with Mississippi John Hurt, his version is actually a cover of the 1900 song by George Sidney and J. Bodewalt Lampe. It's a beautiful melody and a great way to develop your fingerstyle guitar playing.

This song uses a capo, which is an absolutely essential item in my kit bag.

As you probably know, capos raise the pitch of the whole guitar to make it easy to play in different keys, but they also have another advantage. As the frets ascend the guitar neck, the distances between them get smaller. If we can play a piece higher up on the neck, it often means we don't have to stretch as far to reach melody notes and the entire song becomes easier to play. In *Creole Belle*, I place my capo on the 4th fret. This means that even though the first chord I play looks like a C Major, the song is actually in the key of E Major.

This is the first song we've encountered that requires a bit of a stretch from the little finger while holding down a full chord. This is an important technique, but it can feel quite difficult to begin with. For this reason, I've included some short etudes here that will teach you to hold chords, play a boom chick bass line, and stretch out your pinkie to access a hard-to-reach melody note.

Be warned, you may find these etudes a bit harder than the actual song! But don't panic, it's something you can return to in the future if you can't manage all of them now.

In Example 7d, the first position is a barred D6 chord. The first finger barre extends onto the 6th string, so it can take care of two notes in the bassline. Make sure you can play the boom chick bassline cleanly before adding the melody.

The melody is played with the little finger, which first stretches up to the 10th fret, then slides down to the 9th fret. Not only is this a big stretch, it'll try to pull your hand out of position and probably make the rest of the chord buzz. Go slowly, and don't let this worry you at first. Come back to this etude over a series of days and it'll start to get easier.

This is the most difficult position in the etude, so don't get stuck on it. Feel free to leave it out and move to the G Major chord.

On the G Major barre chord, notice that I don't play or fret the note on the A string, and I alter the boom chick pattern to move between just the sixth and fourth string. This is a little secret trick I use all the time, which allows me to play more complicated melodies. It really helps me to reach the high note in the melody.

On the A chord, I use a mini-barre that is played on just the top four strings. The fifth and sixth strings are open, and I use them for the bassline. Again, this makes it a lot easier to reach that high C#. Go slowly through this etude and learn it beat by beat.

Example 7d

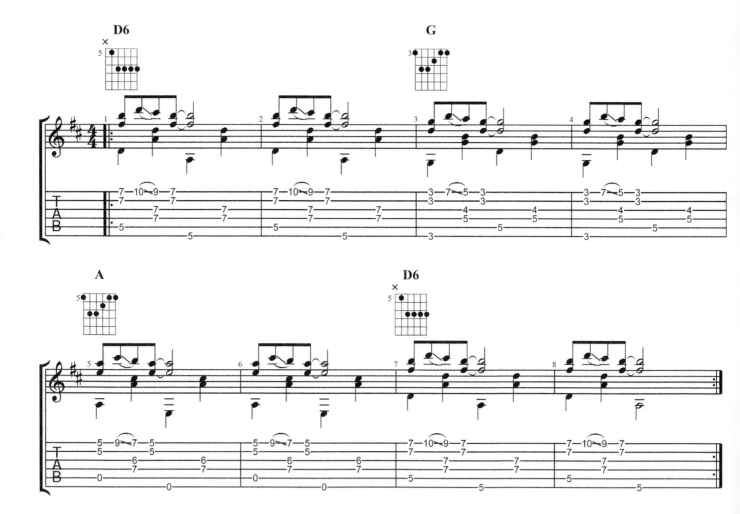

Another technique to look out for is that I play the bass notes of *Creole Belle* by hooking my thumb over the neck of the guitar. Here's an exercise designed to help you get used to it.

There's nothing too difficult here, just fret the bass note with your thumb and use your remaining fingers to form the barre chord.

Example 7e

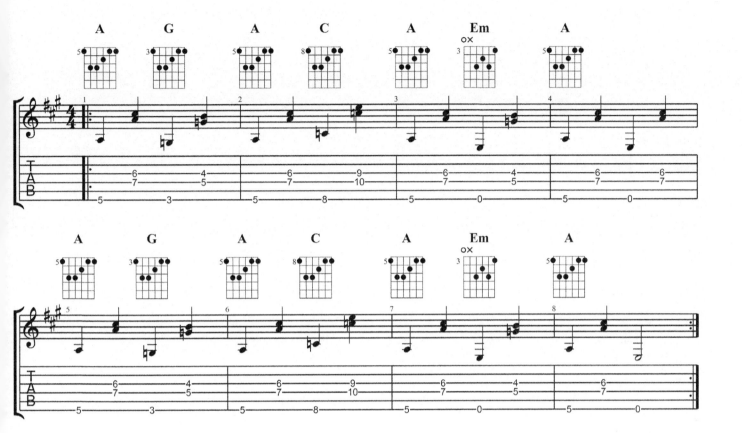

Here's a slightly more syncopated version of the previous exercise to build your finger independence.

Example 7f

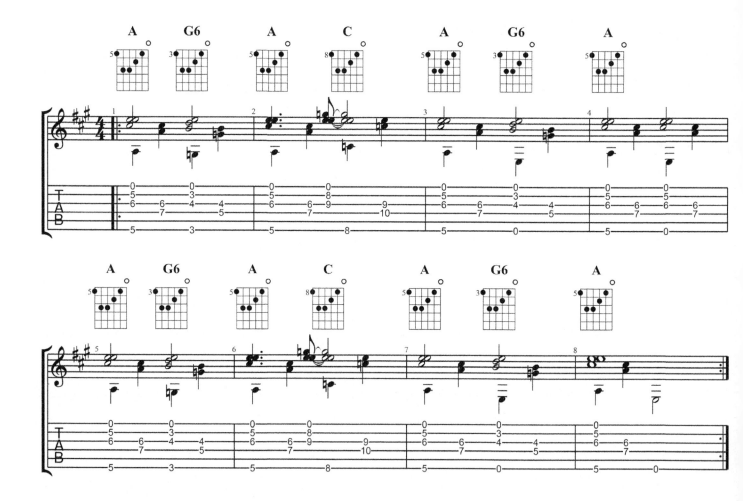

With those preliminaries out of the way, it's time to get to the song.

Bars 1-2:

After the lead-in melody, there are two bars of F Major. I use my thumb to play the root note and use my old trick of fretting both the fifth and fourth strings with my 3rd finger. This allows me to play the boom chick basslines on the bottom three strings. If you can't manage this, feel free to just fret the fourth string and adjust the bassline to use only the sixth and fourth string.

There's a real temptation to play the melody in the second bar with the thumb. You need to resist this and make sure you pick it with your fingers. In the fretting hand, I use my first and fourth fingers to fret the notes.

Bars 3-4:

The melody continues over two bars of C Major. Again, use your first finger and pinkie to fret the melody. The first melody note on the C chord is played on the open third string, and once again there is the temptation to use the thumb to pick it. Don't! Make sure the thumb is playing the boom chick and the picking fingers take care of each melody note.

The final note of the melody is played with a slight bend using your pinkie finger on the fourth string. It's a real challenge to keep the bassline going here, but stick at it, you'll get it!

Bars 5-6:

During two bars of G Major, notice that the boom chick is now played only on the sixth and fourth strings, so you don't need to hold down the rest of the G Major chord. On beat 3 of bar six, the faster rhythm displaces the final melody note and syncopates it against the beat.

Bars 7-8:

We resolve to C Major for one bar before switching to C9 in bar eight. This has an awkward fingering as the second finger needs to take care of both bass notes on the bottom two strings. This is where the earlier exercises will be useful, as you need to stretch out the pinkie to reach the highest note in the song. Again, it's difficult to coordinate this with the boom chick, so go slowly and tackle the song beat by beat.

Bars 9-12:

The second eight bars are almost a direct repeat of the first, with a few alterations to the melody. You shouldn't find anything too troubling here if you can play the first section.

Bars 13-14:

There's a tricky little moment on the C Major chord in bar 14 where I play a faster phrase between the open B string and the 3rd fret on the G string. As always, learning this is simply a case of working through the phrase slowly and syncing the melody with the bassline. As I've mentioned before, look for which melody note syncs with the bassline and fit the others in between.

Bars 15-16:

These are played much the same as bars 7-8 but watch out for the syncopation in bar 15 and the final quick chord change between C Major and F Major in bar 16.

Example 7g – Creole Belle

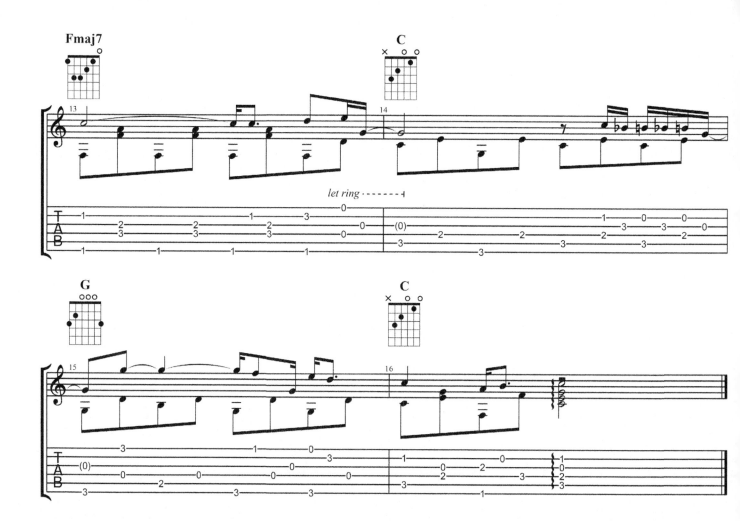

Conclusion and Final Words

Congratulations Thrill Seekers, we made it!

In this book, I've taught you all the skills and concepts you need to become a great fingerstyle guitarist. I've broken it down for you, piece by piece, then brought it all back together to show you how to play some awesome songs. But this is just the start. It's up to you to stay hungry and seek out the music you want to learn.

When tackling a tune, break it down beat by beat, memorize it, and gradually add it to your arsenal. No one's going to do that for you, so if you're going to progress, you're going to have to have the self-motivation and discipline to push yourself forward. Learning fingerstyle guitar is a lot of fun and extremely satisfying, so I promise you, all your hard work will be worth it.

I want to mention *repetition* one last time. Repetition is not only your main tool for getting better at playing pieces, it's for remembering them too. You have memory in your brain, but you also have memory in your fingers and body. Muscle memory must be programmed *slowly* and *carefully*. Once it's been developed though, you'll never forget it! Work hard on repetition, it will help you become a much better player.

Find a quiet place to practice. You're going to be repeating each piece of music beat by beat, bar by bar, and other people may not want to hear it! Take your guitar to your practice room and develop your skills in a distraction-free environment. There's no need to practice in front of others, but when you come out of your practice room, be ready to dazzle them with your skills!

Be thorough. Go over the exercises, songs and techniques in this book again. Seek out more songs and techniques. Break them down and repeat them until they're in your muscle memory, then get playing!

It's been so much fun writing this book and I hope it's unlocked some of the mystery of fingerstyle guitar for you. You're like an uncaged animal – the door's been opened and now you're out in the real world! You're going to have a great time working out arrangements of your favorite songs with the skills that you've learnt.

I hope to see you at a gig somewhere down the endless road.

Take care and have fun!

Jerry Emmanuel cgp

Printed in Great Britain
by Amazon